GRADUATE THEOLOGICAL FOUNDATION

Early Christian Worship

Oscar Cullmann

 Wyndham Hall Press

EARLY CHRISTIAN WORSHIP

by

Oscar Cullmann

Reproduced from EARLY CHRISTIAN WORSHIP, by Oscar Cullman. (c) SCM Press Ltd. 1953. Reproduced by permission of The Westminster Press, 925 Chestnut Street, Philadelphia, PA 19107.

Library of Congress Catalog Card Number

87-051009

ISBN 1-55605-018-6

Printed in the United States of America

Under the sponsorship of the Graduate Theological Foundation, this book is distributed by Wyndham Hall Press, Post Office Box 877, Bristol, Indiana 46507.

CONTENTS

I BASIC CHARACTERISTICS OF THE EARLY CHRISTIAN SERVICE OF WORSHIP

II THE GOSPEL ACCORDING TO ST. JOHN AND EARLY CHRISTIAN WORSHIP

I

BASIC CHARACTERISTICS OF THE EARLY CHRISTIAN SERVICE OF WORSHIP

1. THE SOURCES

OUR sources for the investigation of the early Christian service of worship do not yield a perfectly clear picture of the outward development of the gatherings for worship; they do disclose, however, a fairly clear tendency in worship. Our concern in the following pages will be to show what this tendency is.

The passages which serve as our main sources are these; the description of the life of the community in the Book of Acts (2.42 and 46; 5.42), and the statements of Paul in 1 Corinthians (especially chap. 14; also chap. 11.20 ff) and to these we must add all the greetings formulae and doxologies of the New Testament Epistles. A further important mine of information is the Book of the Revelation of St. John, for it is not without significance that the Seer mentions that he saw his visions on a 'Lord's Day' (1.10), at a time, therefore, when the Christian community was gathered together. Thus he sees the whole drama of the last days in the context of the early Christian service of worship which, so to speak, has its counterpart and at the same time its fulfilment in the coming aeon, so that all that takes place in the gatherings of the early Christian community, seen from this side, appears as an anticipation of that which in the last day takes place from God's side. Hence the whole Book of Revelation from the greeting of grace and peace in chapter 1.4 to the closing prayer: Come Lord Jesus, in chapter 22.20, and the benediction in the last verse, is full of allusions to the liturgical usages of the early community. We shall further seek to establish in the next chapter that in a special way the Gospel of John is outstandingly valuable as a

7

source for the question of the early Christian service of worship.[1]

In addition to these main sources in the New Testament we have at our disposal Christian literature to the year 150. This material is, for our purpose, all the more to be consulted since, particularly where a text has references to worship and liturgy, the elements attested in the text are much older than this text itself. Of these extra-canonical, early Christian documents the most important for our problem is the *Didache*, which contains the earliest Christian collection of liturgies. As the conclusion of the development with which we are here concerned we may examine the important account of the apologist Justin in his first Apology, where for the first time the order of service is described in detail in a manner which enables us to draw conclusions concerning the whole early Christian period.[2] Lastly we must mention here among the sources a pagan document also: the letter of the governor Pliny to the Emperor Trajan, where, in connexion with the question of the treatment of the Christians by the State, some facts are given about the usages in the services of worship of these Christians, the facts as collected, and understood by a heathen official.[3]

H. Lietzmann[4] has laid it down as basic principle of historical method in liturgics that the starting point be made in the later sources and from there the way back be sought to the time of the first beginnings where the sources are few and far between and development is still going on. Although this method is on the whole to be approved, warning must be given of the dangers of a too one-sided application of it. It carries with it very easily the temptation to want to find willy nilly later developments in earliest times, at least in embryo. In order to

---

[1] See below p. 37 ff.

[2] See English translation below p. 30, note 1.

[3] Pliny the Younger, *Epist.* X, 96 ff. For translation of the important para. 7 see below p. 22, note 3.

[4] H. Lietzmann, *Messe und Herrenmahl. Eine Studie zur Geschichte der Liturgie*, 1926.

avoid this danger we shall first simply bring together individually the different elements of the services of worship from the earliest times in the more or less unconnected manner in which they have been handed down to us, and without endeavouring to systematize them in relation to one another. Later, of course, we shall have to put forward the questions which arise at that very point, namely, How were these elements connected with one another? What was the mutual relation in this system between the liturgical order and the freedom of the working of the Spirit? What constitutes the fundamental and specifically Christian character of the early Christian service of worship?

2. PLACE AND TIME

In the first part of the Book of Acts we find that the first Christians gathered in the Temple (2.46 and 5.42; also Luke 24.53) in accordance with the Jewish custom, just as Jesus himself in Jerusalem had taught daily in the Temple (Mark 14.49).[1] But we hear also how, in this very respect—*in respect of place*—the gatherings of the Christian community were growing above and beyond the limits of their Jewish setting; for at the same time the disciples were coming together in particular houses; in an upper room (1.13), probably in the same room in which Christ appeared on Easter Sunday while the disciples were at their meal (Luke 24.33) and in the house of the mother of John Mark (Acts 12.12) in which Jesus had perhaps also taken the last meal with his disciples before his death. The house which figures in the story of Pentecost might be the same house. It is possible that in Acts 2.46 and 5.42 the expression κατ' οἶκον is really to be translated by the

[1] E. Lohmeyer, *Die Reinigung des Tempels (Theologische Blätter*, 1941, Sp. 257 ff) shows on the other hand how the cleansing of the Temple as an eschatological act has the sense of fulfilling the expectation at the last day of a 'house of prayer for all peoples'—which is then realized in another way in the Lord's Supper 'for the many', i.e. for the peoples.

plural 'alternately in their houses', so that several private houses had served as gathering places for the Jerusalem community. This is, however, to say the least, doubtful. Alongside ἐν τῷ ἱερῷ 'in the Temple' it can easily mean 'at home', just as the house community which gathered in the home of Aquila and Priscilla in Ephesus and Rome (1 Cor. 16.19; Rom. 16.5) and that which gathered in Colossae in the home of Philemon (Philem. 2) and in Laodicea in the home of Nympha (Col. 4.15) are designated as ἡ κατ' οἶκον ἐκκλησία[1] (the church that is in the home). Special importance was attached in early Christianity to the fact that the whole community should gather in *one* place (ἐπὶ τὸ αὐτό—in the same place). Separate gatherings were rejected.[2]

Concerning the time of the gatherings Acts says that they took place daily (2.46 and 5.42, see also Luke 24.53). The Sabbath too may still have been observed here and there.[3] Here however we affirm, as we did in the paragraph concerning *place*, that already in earliest times the primitive Christian (Church) service created for itself a specifically Christian setting in which *one* day was specially marked out as the day for the (Church) services—the Lord's Day.[4] That is not the Jewish Sabbath, but in deliberate distinction from Judaism, the first Christians selected the first day of the week, since on this day

[1] A house community is also presupposed in Romans 16.23.
From later times we hear that in Gentile Christian churches the triclinium was used for classrooms and for meetings for worship (*Acta Petri cum Simone*, chap. 21. Lipsius-Bonnet I, 68 and *Acta Thomae*, chap. 131). These rooms could of course, accommodate only a limited number of believers. According to the *Acta Saturnini*, chapter 2, 47 persons were assembled in a private house in Abitina.

[2] 1 Cor. 11.20 ff. Ignatius of Antioch particularly is always giving warnings against such separate gatherings. See *Eph.* 5.2; *Magn.* 7,1; *Trall.* 7,2; *Philad.* 4; *Smyrn.* 8,1; 9,1.

[3] Whether, however, as H. Lietzmann, *Geschichte der alten Kirche*, 1932, p. 57 supposes, Matt. 24.20 can be quoted as confirmation is very questionable. The words μηδὲ σαββάτῳ, which are wanting in Mark 13.18, can just as well be left out in Mark as added in Matthew.

[4] 1 Cor. 16.2; Acts 20.7; Rev. 1.10; *Didache* 14,1; Ignatius, *Magn.* 9,1; *Barnabas* 15.9; Justin, *Apol.* I, 67,3; *Letter of Pliny* X, 96,7 (by *status dies* here Sunday is certainly meant).

Christ had risen from the dead, and on this day he had appeared to the disciples gathered together for a meal.

The Lord's Day of the first Christians was therefore a celebration of Christ's resurrection. *Each* Lord's Day was an Easter Festival, since this was not yet confined to one single Sunday in the year. This meaning of Sunday is repeatedly forgotten today. We are dealing here with a specifically Christian festival day, and the fact that it derives its meaning from Christ's resurrection, gives us an important hint as to the basic Christian meaning of all gatherings of the primitive community for worship.[1] In the very earliest period, indeed, there is not yet any special name for this day. It is still called 'the first day of the week', according to the Jewish system of chronology. As such it appears in the Gospel accounts of the resurrection. The Apostle Paul, also, uses this name in 1 Cor. 16.2, where he requests the Corinthians to lay aside on that day something for the collection. Acts (20.7) recounts in the 'we' passages, that the gathering for breaking of bread, at which Paul preached till midnight, took place 'on the first day of the week'. It is in the Book of the Revelation of St. John (1.10) that we first come across the specifically Christian name 'the Lord's Day', (likewise in *Didache* 14,1). At the same time we must realize that by 'Lord', Christ is meant and not God. It is Christ's Day, the day of Christ's resurrection. When today we say Sunday is the 'Day of the Lord' (cf. French *dimanche* from *dominica*) we are inclined to interpret it as God's Day in the light of the Old Testament commandment about the Sabbath. It is correct to say that from the time of Christ's resurrection, the day of rest appointed by God was transferred to the day of Christ's resurrection and was regarded as 'fulfilled' in it; nevertheless it must not be forgotten that for purposes of Christian worship it was first and foremost the day on which Jesus rose from the dead, (*Barnabas* 15.9). Later,

---

[1] Later in Tertullian (*De corona mil.*, chap. 3) the joy of the resurrection gains expression in that one does not kneel at prayer or fast on that day.

full use was made of the symbolism of the heathen sun cult bound up with this day, in so far as there was recognized in it a symbol of the resurrection, and this led to the circulation of the term Sunday in Christian circles (first attested in Justin's *Apology* 1, 67, 3) and to the raising of this day to the status of an official holiday under Constantine the Great[1] with his leanings towards syncretism. All that, however, does not detract one whit from the exclusively Christian origin of Sunday in the early community.

3. The Several Component Parts

What, then, are the essential component parts of the service of worship celebrated in these gatherings? First of all we are bound to say that they are extraordinarily *manifold* and that the worship life of our Church in contrast seems remarkably impaired. In the Book of Acts (2.42 and 46; 20.7) instruction, preaching, prayer and breaking of bread are mentioned, and mentioned in such a way as clearly to show that these elements were, from the beginning, the foundation of all the worship life of the Christian community.

What our conception of *preaching* should be can be gathered from the examples in the Book of Acts. Above all we notice in these examples a concern to trace the history of salvation from the Old Testament to the event of Christ in the present.

The *prayers* are partly free, adapted to the circumstances, and were evidently regarded, not exclusively but mainly, as the prophet's business, in accordance with *Didache* 10,6: 'The prophets are allowed to give thanks as much as they want.' At the same time, however, at an early date the Lord's Prayer appears to have been said in the service, as is clearly indicated by the addition of the Doxology shortly afterwards (*Didache* 8), which represents the liturgical echo of the congregation, so to

[1] See Felix Stähelin—*Constantin der Grosse und das Christentum.* (*Zeitschrift für Schweiz. Gesch.* 1937, p. 385 ff.)

speak, to the prayer taught by Jesus.[1] The fact that in Gala-
tians 4.6 and Romans 8.15 all prayer is designated as a 'saying
Abba' seems also to connect with the liturgical use of the Lord's
Prayer (Our Father).[2] In the *First Epistle of Clement*, in chapters 59-61, we have the example of a liturgical congregational
prayer as used about the year 96—an established element of
the worship of the Roman Church.

For the oldest liturgical prayers, however, we must go to
the prayer preserved in the Aramaic *Maranatha*: 'Come Lord
Jesus.' The Greek translation at the end of the Book of
Revelation (22.20) shows that *Maranatha* is an imperative,[3]
that is to say a prayer, and not an indicative: 'our Lord is
coming.' This call in prayer stands in the Aramaic form at the
end of the Epistle to the Corinthians (16.22). From the *Didache*
we discover that it was said in particular at the end of the meal
in connexion with the eucharistic liturgy (chap. 10,6). The fact
that this prayer is handed down by Paul untranslated and that
it continued in that original form until the time of the composition of the *Didache* shows the extraordinarily important
rôle which this oldest liturgical prayer of the early Christian
community must have played. The *Didache* has handed down
to us other eucharistic prayers which have almost word for
word parallels in Judaism. In the *Maranatha* prayer, on the
other hand, we come right down to the specifically Christian
element in early liturgical prayer, an element which connects
closely with the fact that the day of the Christian service of
worship is the day of Christ's resurrection. On this day Christ

[1] The words 'for thine is the kingdom' etc. are, as is well known, not spoken
by Jesus but are introduced into late mss. in the Matthean text of the Lord's
Prayer under the influence of early Christian liturgy. E. Lohmeyer also, *Das
Vaterunser*, 1946, p. 173, suspects that the Lord's Prayer was originally said at
the celebration of the Meal and for that reason a formula of praise is added.

[2] These Pauline passages presuppose the simple address 'Father' as in the
Lucan text of the Lord's Supper (πάτερ Luke. 11.2). 'Our Father' as in Matthew
would be in Aramaic not *abba* but *abbun*.

[3] It is not disputed that on purely linguistic grounds the form can be equally
well translated as an indicative. See K. G. Kuhn in *Th. Wb. z. N.T.* III, p. 500.

appeared at a meal with the disciples. So now he ought to appear again, in the Christian celebration of the Meal, since, 'where two or three are gathered together in my name, there am I in the midst of them' (Matt. 18.20). This presence in the Spirit in the congregation is, however, an earnest of his coming at the End. This ancient prayer thus points at the same time backwards to Christ's appearance on the day of his resurrection, to his present appearance at the common meal of the community and forwards to his appearance at the End, which is often represented by the picture of a Messianic meal. In all three cases a meal is involved. Therefore the *Maranatha* is above all a eucharistic prayer.[1]

* * *

That brings us to the 'breaking of bread', this characteristic expression of early Christian worship. Space forbids us to deal with the whole complex problem of the relation of the Lord's Supper in the first community to Jesus' Last Supper.[2] I should like to refer only to the points which come into consideration in a general review of the worship life of the primitive community. It may be taken as agreed that the oldest celebrations of the Lord's Supper took place in the setting of an actual meal,[3] in which the drinking of wine was not absolutely necessary as we find from Acts, which speaks only of 'breaking of bread' and of nothing else. The fact that one says 'breaking of bread' and not 'eating of bread'—an unusual expression to designate a meal[4]—indicates, of course, that those present were conscious of performing at the same time an act of special

---

[1] The German grace: '*Komm Herr Jesu, sei unser Gast*' can therefore in a certain sense be regarded as a faithful translation of the *Maranatha*.

[2] I refer the reader here to the well informed study of E. Gaugler, *Das Abendmahl im Neuen Testament*, Basel, 1943.

[3] *Didache* 10,1 'after you are satisfied with food.'

[4] See J. Weiss. *Das Urchristentum*, 1917, p. 41.—cf. also J. Behm in *Th. Wb. z. N.T.* Vol. III, p. 727 ff.—J. Jeremias, *Die Abendmahlsworte Jesu*, 2nd ed. 1949. p. 64 f actually regards the term as a pseudonym, which should conceal the secret of the Lord's Supper from the heathen.

significance. The connexion with the blood and in general with the death of Christ seems here to be missing. It is an essential characteristic of this meal that, as Acts 2.46 has it, 'exuberant joy' prevailed amongst them.[1] This was not aroused primarily by the remembrance of the Last Supper, but is explained in the first instance by the remembrance of those other occasions where Jesus, immediately after his resurrection, appeared to the disciples, while they were having a meal. According to Luke 24.36 the eleven ate with the Risen Christ on Easter Sunday after Jesus (Luke 24.30) had also broken bread with two disciples on the road to Emmaus shortly before. In Luke 24.36 as in the narrative in John 21.12 ff, the meal taken with the risen Christ consists of fish. This may to some extent account for the fact that later the symbol of the fish was associated with the Eucharist,[2] though the symbol certainly has other roots besides this. That also points to the connexion between the early Christian celebration of the Lord's Supper and the Easter appearances of Christ at meals.

If, then, the first appearances of the risen Christ took place during meals, we must take into consideration, much more than is generally done, the fact that *the first eucharistic feasts of the community look back to the Easter meals,* in which the Messianic Meal promised by Jesus at the Last Supper was already partly anticipated.[3] Just how closely the thought of the resurrection in general was linked with the recollection of those Easter meals shared with the Christ of the appearances can be gauged from Acts 10.40, where in Peter's address we read: 'This Christ God raised up the third day and gave him to be made

[1] See the expression ἀγαλλίασις. R. Bultmann shows in *Th. Wb. z. N.T.* Vol. I p. 19, that it is especially 'eschatological' joy that is meant by this word. In Corinth this appears to have degenerated to such a degree that they got drunk. (1 Cor. 11.23.)

[2] See reproduction in F. J. Dölger, *Die Fischdenkmäler in der frühchristlichen Plastik und Kleinkunst,* 1928.

[3] In my essay 'La signification de la Sainte Cène dans le christianisme primitif' (*Revue d'Histoire et de Philosophie* rel., 1936, p. 1 ff). I have taken pains to bring forward thorough-going proofs of this.

manifest, not to all the people but unto witnesses that were chosen before of God, even to us *who did eat and drink with Him after He rose from the dead.*' Acts 1.4 refers also to the 'eating together' with the risen Christ, for the expression συναλιζάμενος which is always wrongly translated: '(the risen Christ) was assembled together with them', means more precisely: 'He took salt with them.' The Latin, Syriac and Coptic translations have actually rendered this word here 'eat together'.[1]

The 'rejoicing' at the eucharistic meals is thus to be explained from the connexion of this celebration with the thought of the resurrection on the one hand, and on the other hand from the connexion with the thought of the Messianic meal.[2] The eucharistic meal of the community, which is gathered in Jesus' name and at which consequently he is now effectively present in the πνεῦμα (Spirit) occupies its appointed place between Christ's resurrection meal and the expected eschatological meal. What we said about the threefold coming of Christ in our discussion of *Maranatha* proves true therefore for the celebration of the Lord's Supper as such. The coming of Christ into the midst of the community gathered at the meal is an anticipation of his coming to the Messianic meal and looks back to the disciples' eating with the risen Christ on the Easter days. In the Book of Revelation, which, as we know, correlates the present service of worship and its fulfilment in the events of the last days, Christ says: 'Behold I stand at the door and knock. If any man hear my voice and open the door I will come in to him, and will sup with him and he with me.' That is the answer to the old eucharistic prayer: *Maranatha! The prayer is fulfilled already in the community's celebrations of the Lord's Supper.*

The emphasis laid on the presence of the risen Christ at these

[1] In this connexion, it is to be noted also that, in the Jewish Christian *Pseudo-clementine Diamartyria* IV and *Hom.* XIV, 7, the Eucharist is celebrated with bread and salt and actually described as μεταλαβεῖν τῶν ἁλῶν.

[2] Corresponding to the meaning of ἀγαλλίασις see above p. 15.

early meals is in keeping with the fact established above that the first Christians chose the day of Christ's resurrection as the day for the service of worship, and conforms also with the whole central meaning of the prayer *Maranatha*. The term 'Lord's Supper' (1 Cor. 11.20) also points in this direction.

But then Paul in 1 Cor. 11 felt himself obliged to stress, in face of the Corinthian misusages, that the meal celebrated goes back to Jesus' Last Supper before his death.[1] This Last Supper

---

[1] The distinction between the two types of Lord's Supper which H. Lietzmann, *Messe und Herrenmahl*, 1926, traces back into primitive Christianity from the Egyptian Liturgy (*Serapion*) on the one hand and the liturgy of Hippolytus on the other: (1) early communal type of the *Didache*, without any connexion with the death of Christ: (2) Pauline type with a connexion with the death of Christ,—this distinction contains very important elements of truth, but requires however a double supplement: (1) in that, contrary to Lietzmann's view, the common origin of *both* types is to be sought in the historical Jesus' Last Supper, even if only indirectly in the case of the first type: (2) in that the *direct* origin of the first type which Lietzmann unsatisfactorily seeks in the daily table fellowship of the historical Jesus with his disciples is in fact to be found, as we have shown here, in the meal scenes of the period of Christ's post-resurrection appearances.

F.-J. Leenhardt, *Le Sacrement de la Sainte Cène* 1948 p. 64 ff simply identifies my view as developed in the above mentioned essay (see note 3, p. 15) and especially in the present book, with that of H. Lietzmann, although he at least speaks on p. 63 of an 'extension of his construction'. The previous paragraph of this footnote in which I expressly disassociate myself from H. Lietzmann's view, appeared *word for word* in the first edition and likewise my statements made in the text, which can leave little doubt that, for me, in spite of F.-J. Leenhardt's claim to the contrary, 'the last supper of the historical Jesus is in fact the germ cell of the community's meal celebrations' (see above the whole passage!). Because I stress the influence of the Easter meals on the first celebrations of the primitive Church, I restore, in opposition to H. Lietzmann, the connexion with that concept which F.-J. Leenhardt like myself regards as essential for Jesus' completed act namely the eschatological. Admittedly Paul reminded the Corinthians of the meaning for Jesus of his death and also for the primitive community inextricably bound up with it. I have already in the first edition emphasized in spaced type that the Apostle for his part does not mean this emphasis to dispense with the eschatological (see what is said on p. 18). I cannot therefore comprehend how F.-J. Leenhardt on pp. 64 and 65 can ascribe to me (as Lietzmann and Loisy) the opposite view! My task in my works on this subject was not to deal with the whole problem of the Lord's Supper but only with the question of the early Christian celebration. How little in fact my own view of the meaning of Jesus' Last Supper differs from that of F.-J. Leenhardt can be gathered from the above short synopsis which likewise appears in the 1944 edition.

When F.-J. Leenhardt claims on p. 69 that the correlation which I assume

of the historical Jesus is certainly the original source of the community Feast, in so far as it was in remembrance of that Last Supper that the disciples came together after the resurrection to eat the meal at which the risen Christ appeared to them. In Jesus' words at the Last Supper also, as they are reported in the Synoptic Gospels, there is already present the connexion with the thought of the Messianic meal ('till I shall eat it anew') and further with the thought of the new *covenant of communion* which is now founded through the death of Christ. There is no doubt that, in the blinding light of the resurrection, the thought that all this happened through the vicarious death of Christ fell completely into the background in the primitive celebrations of the Lord's Supper, as we have seen. For that reason Paul felt himself obliged to emphasize it again. In doing so, however, he did not drop the eucharistic thoughts of the early community concerning the future coming of Christ and the present fellowship with him already realized in the gathering for a common meal, as happened in the development which later followed. On the contrary in 1 Cor. 11.26 he emphasizes that the eucharistic proclamation of the Lord's death takes place, *'Till he come'*. And in chapter 10 of the same letter to the Corinthians (v. 16) he speaks of the present *eucharistic union* with the spiritual resurrection body of Christ, which is identical with the Church: 'the bread which we break, is it not a communion of the body of Christ? Seeing that there is one bread, we who are many are one body.'

The idea of fellowship realized through the presence of Christ, which is pushed far too much into the background in our present day communion services, is particularly empha-

between Easter Meals, early Christian celebrations of the Lord's Supper and Messianic meal, means an 'overstepping' of the limits of time, I can here only refer him to my book *Christ and Time*, 2nd ed., 1948, in which I show, how the reciprocal action of the various periods of time in all the linearity of the New Testament conception of time which I stress so strongly, is characteristic of the whole early Christian view of salvation history.

sized in the beautiful prayer in the *Didache* which, following Jewish models, runs thus: 'As this broken bread was scattered upon the mountains, but was brought together and became one, so let thy Church be gathered together from the ends of the earth into thy Kingdom' (chap. 9,4). The *Didache* knows moreover only the pre-Pauline type of Lord's Supper celebration, which belongs to the original community where the connexion with Jesus' Last Supper and his death is still absent. The shed blood of Christ first assumes its permanent place in the Eucharist as a result of Paul's referring back to the original source of early Christian meals, namely the Last Supper of the historical Jesus. In time, however, and with further development, the opposite has happened and the death idea is now so onesidedly emphasized that the valuable links which the primitive Lord's Supper preserved with the resurrection, with that meal with the risen Christ, and with the coming of the risen Christ at the last, are lost. Christ's presence is then bound up exclusively with the elements, and the occasion is no longer an actual meal, while in the early community Christ is thought of as *sitting at table with His own* and sharing the meal.

The *Didache* enables us to establish other parts of the oldest *Lord's Supper liturgy* besides the eucharistic prayers. Thus we find (*Didache* 9,5) that, preceding the prayer which leads up to the *Maranatha*, there is pronounced the command: 'Let none eat or drink of your Eucharist except those who have been baptized in the Lord's name. For concerning this did the Lord say "give not that which is holy to the dogs".' In chapter 14,1 we learn further that a *Confession of Sins* must precede the eating of the meal and that none who has a quarrel with a brother may come to the table until he be reconciled. The closing verses of 1 Corinthians, where Paul purposely uses fragments of the oldest eucharistic liturgy, confirm that in this command, which connects with Matt. 5.23—the logion concerning reconciliation before the sacrifice—we are dealing with a fixed practice. In the Pauline passage an analogous command precedes the *Maranatha*; 'if any man loveth not the Lord, let him be anathema'. The liturgical custom of the '*Holy Kiss*' also, which is mentioned in the previous verse (20) and which appears likewise elsewhere in the New Testament as fixed liturgical usage (Rom. 16.16; 1 Thess. 5.26; 2 Cor. 13.12; 1 Pet. 5.14), stems certainly from the eucharistic liturgy of the early community and signifies that before the meal a complete brotherhood should be established, in order that the Lord, for whose coming prayers are made, may really appear among his people. We can see that the whole celebration is directed towards this *climax, where Christ comes in the Spirit to his own.* Lietzmann[1] is quite right in assuming that the liturgy given in *Didache* 10,6 is to be thought of in dialogue form:

THE LEADER: Let grace come and let this world pass away!
THE CONGREGATION: Hosanna to the Son of David!
THE LEADER: If any man be holy, let him come, if any man be not, let him repent! *Maranatha.*
THE CONGREGATION: Amen.

* * *

We know now the basis of early Christian Worship; sermon, prayer and supper. We learn further, however, from the Pauline Epistles that already in the very earliest period the worship life of the community had still other elements. Besides teaching (sermon) Paul mentions in 1 Cor. 14.26 the Psalms, revelation, speaking with tongues and the interpretation of tongues. By *revelation* is meant, as we see from vv. 29 and 32, the *prophecy* of the prophets. This differs from teaching and preaching in that it is not based on a λόγος σοφίας (word of wisdom) and γνώσεως (knowledge) (1 Cor. 12.8), i.e. intelligible exposition of the Word, but on an ἀποκάλυψις (unveiling), i.e. special inspiration; note, of course, that both are thought of as spiritual gifts, *charismata*. At any rate, there is

---

[1] H. Lietzmann, *Messe und Herrenmahl*, p. 237.

room alongside preaching for a perfectly free proclamation in the Spirit, which Paul, of course, insists the community must critically examine (1 Cor. 14.29 and 1 Thess. 5.19: 'Quench not the Spirit; despise not prophesyings; prove all things; hold fast that which is good'). The *Didache*, too, requires the distinction of true and false prophecy (chaps. 11-13).

According to Paul (1 Cor. 14), greater caution is required in handling the practice of speaking with tongues in the service, these inarticulate sounds uttered without understanding. Nevertheless, he allows this quite free working of the Spirit in the gathering for worship as a particular form of prayer, provided someone is there who can make it intelligible, and that it is done in order and can be regarded as serving the purpose of the gathering, the upbuilding of the Church. Where these provisions are not fulfilled, on the other hand, it should be suppressed. Speaking with tongues is perhaps explained as arising from the enthusiasm roused by the experience of Christ's coming in worship in the common meal, by the fulfilment of the *Maranatha*.[1]

We see how perfectly free and unrestricted spiritual utterances have their place alongside fixed liturgical forms. The frequently mentioned *Psalms and Hymns* (apart from 1 Cor. 14.26 especially Col. 3.16 and Eph. 5.19), the use of which in the service was taken over from Judaism, are likewise to be thought of, on the one hand, as free compositions and on the other hand as the repeated pieces of a liturgy. The familiar songs of the early Christian service which are preserved for us again in the Johannine Apocalypse are partly of direct Jewish descent[2] and partly modelled on the Jewish songs. We may mention here the following as the oldest of all Christian songs: Rev. 5.9; 5.12; 5.13; 12.10-12; 19.1-2; 19.6. The so called

---

[1] I am of the opinion that the Pentecost Miracle also (Acts 2) presupposes a similar coming of Christ, so that this need not necessarily be put in the same category as the appearance to more than 500 brethren (1 Cor. 15.5).

[2] Towards the end of the century we discover from Tertullian, *De jejunio*, chapter 13 that at Agapes Psalm 133 was sung.

Odes of Solomon belong also to this early period.[1] The letter of Pliny mentions antiphonal singing, in which the Christians sing before sunrise 'a song to Christ as to a God'. Such passages make it clear that liturgically ordered singing was already in use in these first gatherings.[2]

The letter of Pliny mentions further the commitments entered on by the Christians at their gatherings, 'to commit no theft, no murder, no adultery, not to break their word, not to deny possession of something entrusted to them'.[3] The reference here appears to be to the *Decalogue*, which, in that case, had also found its place in liturgical usage, provided that the references mentioned do not simply imply that part of the Christian sermon in which Pliny, the heathen governor, in view of the complaints against the Christians, was particularly interested.

We may assume with certainty that *Confession formulae* were recited in the early Christian service of worship. The verbs ὁμολογεῖν and ἐξομολογεῖσθαι (confess) (Rom. 10.10; Phil. 2.11, etc.) connect above all with the confession that Christ is the Lord, in the same way as the early liturgical prayer *Maranatha* is concerned with his Second Advent. I have shown elsewhere[4] how, in the New Testament and the other early Christian writings, this confession to the *Kurios* appears in

---

[1] These songs, which were discovered in a Syrian translation by R. Harris and first published in 1909, can be read in a German translation by H. Gressmann in E. Hennecke's *Neutestamentlichen Apokryphen* (2nd ed., 1924) p. 437 ff.

[2] Later we discover from Tertullian, *De orat.*, chapter 27, that the closing verses of the Psalms were sung responsively. On the whole question of the use of music see Markus Jenny, 'Musik und Gottesdienst nach dem Neuen Testament'. (*Musik und Gottesdienst*, 1948, p. 97 ff.)

[3] We reproduce here in translation the whole passage of Pliny's letter pertaining to worship. (Chap. X, 96.7):

'[The Christians we examined] claimed that their entire offence or their entire error was confined to this that they gathered regularly on a fixed day before sunrise to sing antiphonally a song (*carmen*) to Christ as to a god, and to bind themselves an oath not to commit this or that crime but rather to commit no theft, no murder, no adultery, not to break their word, not to deny possession of something entrusted to them. Then it is their custom to disperse and then reassemble to share a common meal together, but an ordinary and innocent affair. . . . '

[4] O. Cullmann, *Les premières confessions de foi chrétiennes*, 2nd ed., 1948.

more detailed formulae also, since there did not yet exist a fixed text. All these old confession formulae have this in common, that they are Christocentric and that they stress the *present Lordship of Christ.* Thus we find confirmed at this point also a characteristic of all expressions used in the service of worship that we have dealt with till now—the characteristic that Christ, the risen Lord, stands right in the centre. We find it stated in the *Didache* (14,1) that there was also a *confession of sin,* even in early times, alongside the confession of faith in connexion with the Lord's Supper.

The New Testament contains, furthermore, numerous formulae of *benediction,* whose stereotyped and solemn character we may explain from their use in the gathering of the community. The benediction formulae at the beginning: 'Grace be with you and peace from God our Father and our Lord and Saviour', are probably the liturgical introductory formulae which were spoken at the beginning of the service. The formulae of benediction which stand at the end of the Epistles: 'The grace of our Lord be with your spirit' (Gal. 6.18; Phil. 4.23) or: 'be with you' (1 Cor. 16.23) or: 'be with you all' (Rev. 22.21) or, also in the fuller tripartite liturgical form: 'The grace of the Lord Jesus Christ and the love of God and the communion of the Holy Ghost be with you all' (2 Cor. 13.13)—these formed probably the transition to the actual breaking of bread.

The exceedingly numerous *doxologies,* which occur at the end of and also within New Testament passages, owe their origin to the service of worship. They have been taken over from Judaism. We have already discussed how the Lord's prayer had found quite early a congregational echo in a doxology. Primitive Christianity did not hesitate to use stereotyped liturgical formulae.[1] In the Pauline Epistles we find such

---

[1] On the question of liturgy see also G. P. Wetter, *Altchristliche Liturgien* I und II, 1921/22. F. J. Dölger, *Sol salutis. Gebet und Gesang im christlichen Altertum,* 2nd ed., 1925. Jacques Marty, 'Etude de textes cultuels de prière contenus dans le Nouveau Testament' (*Revue d'Histoire et de Philosophie* rel., 1929, p .234 ff, 366 ff, 1930, p. 234 ff).

doxologies in great number sometimes with εὐλογητός (blessed) (Rom. 1.25; 9.5; 2 Cor. 11.31; 2 Tim. 4.18; Eph. 1.3), sometimes introduced by the word δόξα (glory) (Rom. 11.36; Gal. 1.5; Phil. 4.20).

The presence of so much that is liturgical here in the Pauline Epistles connects almost certainly with the fact that the Apostle, while writing his letters, had in mind the community assembled for worship. He knows that his letters are read out there, and therefore he adds to them already the liturgical formulae. Lietzmann has rightly pointed out that the closing formulae of the Pauline epistles correspond to the liturgical phrases which we find at the beginning of the old liturgy for the Lord's Supper (see especially 1 Cor. 16.21 ff). The reason for that is that Paul knows that the Lord's Supper will follow immediately after the reading of his letter. He expressly urges the reading of the letter before all the brethren, at the end of the first Epistle to the Thessalonians, and adds to it the eucharistic introductory formula: 'The grace of the Lord Jesus Christ be with you.' He again requests reading of the letter, at the end of the Epistle to the Colossians. In 1 Tim. 4.13 reading aloud is urged on Timothy, along with doctrine and exhortation. It is probable, too, that already in the earliest period, not only Christian writings but also Old Testament writings were read, although the first witness to this is Justin in his first Apology (67), where in the description of the service of worship he says: 'the Memoirs of the Apostles (gospels) or the writings of the prophets were read aloud, as long as time allowed.' By writings of the prophets the books of the Old Testament are probably meant. The reading aloud of the Old Testament is a fixed item in the Jewish synagogue service of worship. But the fact that the reading of a letter of a living apostle of Christ seems to have been given the chief place, at least in the communities founded by Paul, shows again how the Jewish framework was filled.

The liturgical *Amen*, likewise taken over from Judaism, is

said by the congregation, as we see from 1 Cor. 14.16. In general the liturgy in the first congregations is something extraordinarily alive, and liturgical formulae show no sign of being paralysed. All members take part in the liturgy. So in the Book of Revelation the 'Amen' is said by the four living creatures, and Justin mentions in his description of the service (*Apol.* 1,67) that the whole assembled people join in the prayers spoken by the leader by saying the 'Amen'.[1] The antiphonal singing, which we have mentioned before and of which Pliny speaks is, of course, further evidence of the participation of all present in the liturgy.

* * *

There remains now only *Baptism* to mention. Here too there is evidence of a rudimentary liturgy for the very earliest period. The stereotyped usage of the verb κωλύειν (to hinder) in the accounts of Baptism in Acts 8.36; 10.47; 11.17 (also Matt. 3.14 and the gospel of the Ebionites and perhaps Mark 10.13-16) seems to me a certain indication of a liturgical question, which was regularly put when a candidate for Baptism stood before the person administering Baptism; τί κωλύει. What doth hinder so-and-so from being baptized? Or the candidate himself asks: What doth hinder me from being baptized?[2] According to Acts 8.37 ('western' text) the administrant answers: 'If thou believest with all thine heart thou mayest' and then the candidate makes a short confession of Christ: 'I believe that Jesus Christ is the Son of God.' Baptism follows merely on the invocation of the name of Christ.[3] Beyond that the *Didache* (chap. 7) contains directions for the external administration of Baptism, which ought to be done in 'running water'; while dipping in 'other' water, and,

---

[1] See the full text below, p. 30, note 1.
[2] Detailed examination in appendix to O. Cullmann, *Baptism in the New Testament*.
[3] Gal. 3.27; 1 Cor. 1.13; Acts. 2.38; 8.16; 10.48; 19.5.

if need be, in warm water, and, even more, mere sprinkling of the head are permitted only in case of emergency.

4. THE AIM OF THE SERVICE

We are now familiar with the various elements of the service of worship in early Christianity. They are extraordinarily numerous, and it is astonishing how many forms the life of worship in these first Christian communities has assumed. In the light of this wealth of form, we must assert here and now that the services of worship in the Protestant Churches of our own era are very much poorer, not only in respect of the free working of the Spirit, but also in respect of what is liturgical and especially in respect of what is aimed at in the gatherings of the community. The aim is constantly described by Paul as building up of the community (1 Cor. 14). We must not interpret this word in the hackneyed pietist sense of 'uplift', but we have to think of the figure of the *body of Christ*, which must be formed effectually in the community. All the different elements which we have examined individually are subordinated to this purpose, which attains its peak in the 'coming of Christ' in the Lord's Supper. To this aim is due the wealth and the variety of the elements in the early Christian service. But, on the other hand, in view of this aim their use is constantly brought under examination and, if necessary, limited. Paul has also seen this second necessity; he has recognized the danger of this wealth, but he has not thrown away the baby with the bath water. On the contrary, he has preserved everything which can contribute to the 'building up' of the body of Christ.

5. THE INTER-RELATION OF THE VARIOUS ELEMENTS: SERVICE OF THE WORD AND LORD'S SUPPER

Our first question must be: In what way were the various elements related to one another? Was only one of them performed at each gathering? We must first of all remember that at that time considerable freedom prevailed, that there were, indeed, fixed liturgical forms and usages, but that as yet they probably stood in no fixed sequence. One or other therefore might well fall out, especially as the performing of the different parts of the service was regarded as a spiritual gift, as a 'charism', and these *charismata* did not always exist all together in any one community. Nevertheless Paul emphasizes, again with a view to the work of building up the community in its gatherings, how necessary it is that these *charismata* work together (1 Cor. 12.5 ff). Although not all the elements we have enumerated were found at each meeting, nevertheless we must suppose that there were some without which such an 'edifying' (upbuilding) meeting in early Christianity was not thinkable.

It has now become customary, in histories of the early Church and of Liturgy, to distinguish sharply between gatherings for the proclamation of the Word and gatherings for the Lord's Supper, corresponding to the arrangement in Judaism, where synagogue service and temple cult stood side by side. If this were correct it would mean that there had been two essentially different types of gathering for worship. The one had developed exactly after the pattern of the Jewish synagogue service, which was exclusively a service of the Word. In it there had been reading of Scripture, preaching, prayer, blessing and perhaps also singing of Psalms. The breaking of bread, the gathering for the Lord's Supper, is to be thought of as quite separate from this. Only later had the two types of service been joined together. In the works of Justin, who, about the year 150, is the first to give a complete description of a Sunday gathering of the community (*Apol.* 1,67),[1] it seems that the two parts are already united; yet even as early as this we are dealing with a later development.

In accepting an original separation of the two kinds of service however, we are concerned with one of those dogmas

[1] See the text below p. 30, note 1.

which have been so often repeated in the text books that they are now taken as facts which do not require to be established by an examination of the texts.[1] But what do the texts at our disposal teach us about such a separation? Except for the very vague description in Pliny's letter we know of none. Pliny[2] tells us, certainly, that the Christians dispersed after that first gathering before sunrise to come together again later for the Lord's Supper. Although Pliny's whole description is not very clear,[3] nevertheless, here too, it is quite evident that it is a question of two parts of one unified act. Even according to the description in Pliny it is unthinkable that the first part could have taken place without the second, as was possible in the Jewish synagogue service. But now, besides these, and before Pliny's time, we have Christian texts which exclude any systematic distinction between gatherings for the Word and gatherings for the Lord's Supper. Admittedly there are texts which speak only of teaching (Acts 5.42) and others which speak only of breaking bread (Acts 2.46), but that does not mean that we must therefore distinguish between two kinds of gathering.

The *missionary preaching* of the Apostles, which naturally did not take place within the framework of a Lord's Supper, has nothing to do with the worship service of the community. It is not therefore permissible to introduce Acts 5.21 as evidence for a 'service of the Word' within the community.[4] This

---

[1] Especially C. Weizsäcker, *Das apostolische Zeitalter*, 2nd ed., 1892, p. 548 ff. R. Knopf, *Das nachapostolische Zeitalter*, 1905, p. 227 ff. H. Lietzmann, *Geschichte der alten Kirche*, Vol. I, 1932, p. 153 ff, Vol. 2, 1936, p. 121. J. Leipoldt, *Der Gottesdienst der ältesten Kirche*, 1937, *pass.*

[2] See above p. 22, note 3.

[3] Above all it should not be forgotten that his sources are the reports of lapsed Christians and tortured deaconesses.

[4] H. Achelis seeks to do this in *Das Christentum in den ersten drei Jahrhunderten*, 1912, 1st vol., p. 160, 6. Moreover he thinks that the statement ὑπὸ τὸν ὄρθρον (about daybreak) Acts 5.21 can be associated with the phrase *ante lucem* in Pliny's letter (para. 7) and therefore heads the chapter on 'Service of the Word' actually 'the meeting by night'. The confusion between missionary preaching service and the gathering for the community worship is everywhere apparent in Achelis' works and elsewhere.

has already been pointed out in the first edition of the present work and ought to be expressly emphasized to meet the objection which it has called forth. Indeed, there was the so-called service of the Word but it existed as missionary preaching for the conversion of the heathen, not for the 'edification' of the community. The fact that an unbeliever on one occasion comes to a gathering of the community should not mislead us into obliterating the distinction. At any rate the author of the Book of Acts writes in chapter 2.42, that the first Christians 'continued steadfastly in the apostles' doctrine and fellowship, and in breaking of bread and in prayers', and in chapter 20.7 we hear, in the 'we' account, that Paul preached a sermon on the Lord's day at the gathering for breaking of bread, and indeed, an exceptionally long sermon, which lasted till midnight, and that *at the close of it the bread was broken*. Here therefore the situation is quite clear. We have found a convincing argument for the view that as a rule there was no gathering of the community without the breaking of bread and that, even if there had been a service which was exclusively a service of the Word, it would have been in any case an exception; but we must make a further observation. It is not permissible to ascribe only to this hypothetical service of the Word all the other expressions of worship of which Paul speaks in 1 Cor. 14, especially speaking with tongues, interpretation of tongues and prophesying, as is the case in the usual supposition of such a distinction. In fact, speaking with tongues can scarcely be explained as arising out of the synagogue atmosphere of a pure service of the Word; on the contrary it presupposes the climax of the meeting, where at the breaking of bread the prayer *Maranatha*, the prayer for the coming of the Lord, is answered and the presence of Christ is truly experienced as anticipation of his Second Coming at the end of the age.

The Lord's Supper is thus the basis and goal of every gathering. This corresponds to all that we have already determined about the place and time and basic character of the primitive Christian gathering. We have seen that the house of John Mark, which was the meeting place in Jerusalem, was perhaps the same one in which Jesus had taken the Last Supper and where he later appeared to the disciples on Easter Day. We have further seen that the Day of the Lord was set apart as the day of the resurrection of Christ and we know that the breaking of bread among the first Christians stood in closest connexion to the Easter appearances of Christ at a meal time. Likewise in the other parts of the liturgy, confession and prayer, the risen Christ stands in the foreground. His presence in the Church is revealed in the common meal and the enthusiastic speaking with tongues is understood in terms of the experience of his coming.

In the service described by Justin,[1] therefore, we are not dealing with a later development, for here the Eucharist and the other elements of worship, above all the proclamation of the Word, are bound up together. That was certainly the case from the beginning.

A change has taken place, however, by the time of Justin in another connexion, and that in a twofold direction. First of all we find that the free expressions of the Spirit, such as prophesying, speaking with tongues and interpretation of tongues have disappeared. What remains, apart from the Eucharist, appears now, but only now in this later form, as an adaptation of the synagogue service. Here arises for the first time a first part which can be described as proclamation of the

[1] We reproduce the passage here in English translation: 'On the day called after the sun a meeting of all who live in cities or in the country takes place at a common spot and the Memoirs of the Apostles or the writings of the Prophets are read as long as time allows. When the reader is finished the leader delivers an address through which he exhorts and requires them to follow noble teachings and examples. Then we all rise and send heavenwards prayers. And, as said before, as soon as we are finished praying, bread and wine mixed with water are laid down and the leader too prays and gives thanks, as powerfully as he can, and the people joins in, in saying the "Amen"; and now comes the distribution to each and the common meal on the gifts that have been brought and to those who are not present it is sent by the hands of the deacons. . . . '

Word, but which is also only a first *part*. This development is furthered through a second change which now sets in; the Lord's Supper gradually ceases to be a proper meal and tends to become a ritual meal. Thereby it ceases to be the general framework of the whole gathering for worship and becomes a second act which forms, with the first act of proclamation, still only '*one*' service, but which is much less closely bound to it than formerly. This development seems to me, therefore, in direct contradiction of the commonly accepted view, to have taken place not in the direction of a combination of two originally different services but rather in the sense of an at first gradual separation into two acts. These are not however separated at this time, as they are perhaps in our own Church, where the normal service each Sunday is still only a service of the Word, after the manner of the synagogue service, and where a complete Christian service is held only on a few Sundays in the year—even then part of the congregation withdraws before the celebration of the Lord's Supper.

I find in the primitive community only *one* act of worship which took place within the setting of a gathering of the community but not in the setting of the Lord's Supper and that is Baptism. That is because of its special significance; it is essentially once for all and not repeated.[1] Apart from that, it would have been practically impossible to combine Baptism with the Lord's Supper, since it was supposed to be performed by immersion in running water if at all possible. Accordingly, it is not as though early Christianity had known three kinds of service, as we are in the habit of imagining, following the modern example: service of the Word and, alongside of it, Baptism and the Lord's Supper. *It is rather so; in the early Church there are only these two celebrations or services—the common meal, within the framework of which proclamation of the Word had always a place, and Baptism.* This is the reason for the close connexion in early Christianity between Baptism and the

[1] See below p. 109.

Lord's Supper. This association of the *two* sacraments arises
not in some later period, it is present already and quite clearly
in Paul in 1 Cor. 10.1-5 (cloud and sea—meat and drink) and,
as we shall see[1] in the Gospel of John (foot-washing and
spear-thrust).[2]

6. FREEDOM OF SPIRITUAL EXPRESSION AND THE BINDING CHARACTER OF LITURGY

We have already mentioned that the free expressions of the
Spirit had disappeared quite early from the meetings and that
this involved the changes which we have established in Justin.
On the other hand, it is the strength of the earlier service of
worship that here free working of the Spirit and liturgical
restrictiveness still go hand in hand and together serve the
one end, the 'building up' of the community.[3] Admittedly
there were dangers from the beginning; on the one hand of
extinguishing the fire of prophecy, on the other hand of in-
dulging in it uncritically. There was need for a strong sense
of moderation and order, such as Paul possessed in a pre-
eminent way, in order to unify such diverse elements as speaking with tongues and prophecy on the one side and the fixed
acts and forms of liturgy on the other. Paul was able to bring
freedom of the Spirit and the restrictions of liturgy together
in the self-same service because he saw everything in the light
of the one aim: the οἰκοδομή (building up of the Church).
For this reason, he is able to allow speaking with tongues,
under certain conditions, and at the same time to repeat liturgical formulae, without giving rise to anarchy with the one or

---

[1] See below p. 105 ff, 114 ff.

[2] R. Reitzenstein, *Die Vorgeschichte der christlichen Taufe*, 1930, is at pains to
confirm the unity of Baptism and Lord's Supper on grounds pertaining to the
history of religion.

[3] The usual alternative: charismatic or liturgical worship is therefore not
correct for primitive Christianity. Thus H. Lietzmann, *Geschichte der alten Kirche*,
Vol. I, 1932, p. 153, supposes an original complete lack of order which produced
no new and special cult forms but resolved into nothing so that recourse was
now had to the forms of the Hellenistic synagogue worship.

lifelessness with the other. It is precisely in this *harmonious combination of freedom and restriction* that there lies the greatness and uniqueness of the early Christian service of worship. With this high aim of the 'building up' of the community, of the body of Christ, constantly in view, Paul does not fall into the error of reducing the worship life of the Church to a minimum from fear of the binding character of liturgy, nor yet does he, out of fear of sectarianism, fall into the error of eliminating on principle from the service of worship all free expressions of the Spirit. Had it been possible to maintain this harmony in the service of worship the formation of sects and groups would have been most effectively checked.

7. THE CHRISTIAN CHARACTER OF THE SERVICE

We come to the last question, which has already emerged at various points in connexion with our examination and which has already found a partial answer in our discussion of the individual parts of the service. What is the *basic* and *specifically Christian* character of the service of the primitive community? We have seen that the individual elements of the outward form arose out of Judaism. Further it is possible that pagan influences as well came in here and there. Nevertheless, both the determination and realization of the aim of the early Christian gatherings represent something quite new which can be properly grasped only from the standpoint of Christian faith.

First, what was the specifically Christian *aim* of the gathering for worship? The occasions serve for the 'building up' of the community as the *Body of Christ*, the spiritual body of the risen Lord. The Church as the body of this Christ must take shape in the gatherings of the community. The Church is built up in virtue of its coming together. But because the Church, which is thus built up, is the spiritual body of the risen Christ himself, we can also say that Christ is shown forth in the gath-

ering of the community: where two or three are gathered in
Christ's name, there is Christ in the midst of them and, indeed,
in such a way that he takes form in the gathering itself. Everything which furthers a 'building up', so understood, and only
this, belongs to the Christian service of worship. This aim
purifies the Christian service of those elements which serve
only to satisfy profane, egocentric human needs, but at the
same time excludes all excessive enthusiasm which would
empty the service in its attempt to purify. The purpose of
building up the Church as the body of Christ is served by all
the different parts we have identified in the early Christian
gatherings: breaking of bread, reading, proclamation, confession, prayer, doxology, blessing, hymns in liturgical and
free form; prophecies, speaking with tongues and interpretation of tongues subjected to examination. It is not as though
in all this only man as such acted. The assembled community
is much more the organ which Christ employs in order to
show forth his body as the Church. For this reason special
gifts of the Spirit are required in the performance of those
various elements of worship and the gathering for worship is
in reality a gift of God to men. Not only in speaking with
tongues is it the spirit which 'groaneth' (Rom. 8.26), but in all
prayer and confession, praise, singing and especially in the
communal breaking of bread it is the Lord who acts.

Two main features of the purpose of all early Christian
gatherings for worship must still be stressed. First, the *Lord's
Supper* is the natural climax towards which the service thus
understood moves and without which it is not thinkable, since
here Christ unites himself with his community as crucified and
risen and makes it in this way one with himself, actually builds
it up as his body (1 Cor. 10.17). Corresponding to this all the
other parts of the service have the *risen Lord of the Church* as
their object. For this reason the day of the Lord's resurrection
is the Christian festive day. For this reason too, all proclamation is intended to awaken and strengthen faith in this Lord

on the basis of his death and resurrection. All reading of Scripture points to this Lord. The confession of faith is a confession to the present Lord, to the *Kurios*. The confession of sins is effectual in view of the work of reconciliation accomplished by the Lord. Prayer is above all prayer for the coming of the Lord, for his coming at the end, but also for his coming in the assembled community, the anticipation of his coming in revealed glory at the last day.

The second main Christian feature of the early service is shown to us in the fact that the risen and present Lord of the Church who stands in the centre of the Christian gathering, points at one and the same time backwards to the crucified and risen historical Jesus and forwards to the coming Christ: what makes the service a real act of worship is the *Holy Spirit*. That is the characteristic of the Holy Spirit in the New Testament view, that he determines the *present* in the time sequence of God's act of salvation, but in such a way that, on the basis of what has happened in Christ in the past, he anticipates already the future, the last things. This character of the Holy Spirit is now most clearly revealed in the early Christian service, for here, through the merits of Christ, everything is fulfilled which was accomplished in the past history of salvation—and which will be achieved in the future. That is why the seer in the Revelation of St. John sees worship and eschatological event together. It is because the Holy Spirit provides this future element, the 'earnest', the essence of all early Christian worship, that the acts of worship mentioned in 1 Cor. 12.5 ff are brought into such close relationship with spiritual gifts. Therein lies the reason for the importance of leaving room for the free working of the Spirit. Early Christian worship is worship in the Spirit (John 4.23). Through him the community is built up into the Body of Christ.

The Holy Spirit, as Christians understood him, is to be found in the Christian Church and manifests himself there in the gatherings for worship of the very early Church. Indeed the highly-developed, hellenistic mystery religions also know a spirit, but it is for them transcendence which penetrates immanence. In Christianity the Spirit is the future which in virtue of the past actualizes itself in the present. This time-character of the Holy Spirit, connecting him with the history of salvation, manifests itself in the very essence of the Christian service, where it is no myth that is represented, but the Christ event of the present is closely bound up with the historical facts of past time and the facts of the last days still in the future.

II

THE GOSPEL ACCORDING TO ST. JOHN AND EARLY CHRISTIAN WORSHIP

PRELIMINARY REMARKS

NEW Testament scholars have recognized for a long time now that the Book of the Revelation of St. John contains much liturgical material belonging to the worship life of early Christianity, so that one may use this New Testament document as a source book for the study of this subject, especially for the study of Christian hymns of the early period.[1] One might say that the seer, who has his visions on a Lord's day, when the Christian community is assembled, treats the early Christian service of worship as an anticipation of the events of the last day, so that he can draw on expressions and images from worship and use them to describe the essentially indescribable drama of the last days.

The Epistle of John also, in its content and style, is only understandable, it seems to me, when its liturgical interest is recognized.

Our aim in the following chapters is to submit the proof that there can be traced in the Gospel of John a distinct line of thought connecting with the service of worship. Scholars have long ago observed and commentators fittingly commented upon the author's deep interest in the sacraments, in this or that passage. We mean to go further, however, and to show how the Gospel of John regards it as one of its chief concerns to set forth the connexion between the contemporary Christian worship and the historical life of Jesus. First of all we shall show that this is a particular aspect of the entire perspective in which John's Gospel places the account of the incarnate Logos, in that it seeks to point to the full identity of

[1] See above page 7.

37

the Lord, present in the early Christian congregation, with the historical Jesus, and to do so in terms of the facts of Jesus' life. It traces the line from the Christ of history to Christ the Lord of the community, in which the Word continually becomes flesh.

1. THE EVANGELIST'S PURPOSE

At the end of his Gospel (chap. 20.30), the author writes that he could tell of many other σημεῖα (signs) of Jesus, which are not written in his book. In these words the author himself implicitly raises the question as to the principles which govern his *choice* of narratives, since he clearly implies that he had at his disposal a far richer tradition about the life of Jesus. Why did he take up the pen at all to write a Gospel when so many were already written? We are not dependent upon a hypothesis in order to answer this question, for, in the following verse of the same passage, he gives us the answer himself: 'These signs are written *that ye might believe that Jesus is the Christ, the Son of God....*' The evangelist tells us himself therefore that his choice has been governed not by a historical principle but by an ecclesiastical or theological principle where the faith of his readers is kept in view. Is there any justification then for the common assertion that the fourth evangelist has no interest in the historical Jesus? The error of this conclusion ought to be stressed right at the outset, since the theological principle he offers, 'Jesus is the Christ', has quite plainly history as its subject. If one speaks of Jesus, one speaks of history. The theological assertion contained in the word 'Christ' is connected, then, with Jesus, with history. Faith in the Jesus of history as the 'Christ' is what the evangelist seeks to impart to his readers; that is the purpose of his writing a 'Life of Jesus'.

He has presented this life in such a way that the connexion between the Jesus of history and the 'Christ' should be clear.

The 'Christ' is, however, the mediator of God's *entire* plan of salvation in past, present and future. The presentation of that quite short period, in which Jesus moved on this earth, is conformed, therefore, to this purpose so as to bring into relief the relation of that once-for-all event to the plan of salvation, which embraces the whole of God's time. That being so, the present in this history of salvation, in which the author and his readers live after Jesus' resurrection, plays an all-important part, since the ultimate aim of this whole literary undertaking is that they should have faith now in this *post-paschal present*.

The purpose of the evangelist, in the general form in which it is expressed above can of course be applied to all the canonical gospels, that is, to the synoptics as well as St. John. Form criticism, as we know, teaches us that the Gospels are not biographies but documents bearing witness to the incarnate Jesus, which stem from faith and seek to lead to faith. The difference between the synoptics and John's Gospel is that the synoptic tradition is the collective work of the community of the faithful, while in John's Gospel we are dealing with a more individual and consciously confessional witness. It is therefore right and proper for us to ask here what particular view of faith in Christ is intended.

None of the other three evangelists speaks so often of the belief or unbelief of the visual and aural witnesses to the deeds and words of Jesus, and this happens always with reference to the purpose expressed in the closing verses. The Johannine concept of faith stands in *closest relationship to the composition of the gospel*. The author is interested in the question of the 'theory of cognition', so to speak, which is posed by such an understanding of the events of the life of Jesus. He is interested in the question, how it is possible that he himself can write a life of Jesus from this particular point of view and how the reader is capable of understanding it. How can the deep-rooted connexion between God's plan of salvation in past, present and future and the once and for all historical character of these events be comprehended? In other words, how can *seeing* be *believing*? We shall later maintain that believing must be followed by the deeper *understanding* which will be possible only after the glorification of Christ.

The relationship of seeing and believing, with reference to the life of Jesus, is therefore a major problem in this gospel.[1] We meet the two words 'seeing' and 'believing' at every turn, so to speak, in John's Gospel. We hear as early as the prologue: 'We have seen his glory' (chap. 1.14), and the book reaches its climax in the account of the Apostle Thomas. We cannot overstress the point that it is not by chance that this is the *last* narrative of the Gospel proper—for chapter 21 is certainly an addition—and it has not been sufficiently recognized that the last words of Jesus which stand in the Fourth Gospel are these words to Thomas, our chapter 20.29: '*because thou hast seen me, thou hast believed. Blessed are they that have not seen, and yet have believed.*'

The evangelist has placed these words at the end of the book, as the crown of his whole work, since his readers are among those who have not seen and yet *ought to believe. The problem raised by this situation underlies the whole Gospel.*

The author does not claim by any means that eyewitness is of no account. The words in the Prologue about those who have seen the glory are in accordance with the words at the end of the Gospel just mentioned. It is obvious that there were those in Jesus' lifetime who first of all saw and that all of a later day, who have not themselves seen, can seek support in the witness of those who actually did see with their own eyes. (1 John 1.1 ff.) But it is not sufficient to seek support in an eyewitness, however necessary that may also be. There must be added to this an act of faith, which a deeper understanding of the life of Jesus presupposes. In this respect readers are in exactly the same situation as the evangelist himself.

[1] See also in O. Cullmann. Εἶδεν καὶ ἐπίστευσεν *La vie de Jésus objet de la vue et de la foi d'après le quatrième Evangile in Mélanges offerts à Maurice Goguel*, 1950.

We find therefore in the Fourth Gospel, on the one hand passages which stress the necessity of *seeing* and, on the other hand, passages which stress the necessity of *believing*. As in the first Epistle of John, so also in the Gospel the three verbs ὁρᾶν (see—with its synonyms), πιστεύειν (believe) and γιγνώσκειν (know) stand in closest relationship (chap. 14.7, 9, 17).[1] At first sight it seems a contradiction to say, on the one hand, that seeing is what matters, on the other hand, that not seeing but believing is what matters. Attempts are often made to explain away the apparent contradiction by saying that in the first case a purely spiritual seeing is meant. The Johannine use of the three synonyms ὁρᾶν, θεωρεῖν and θεάομαι argues patently against this. It can, admittedly, be proved that the last two may also carry the meaning of a spiritual seeing, but not only does the Johannine use of the three verbs show that all three are virtually synonymous (cf. θεᾶσθαι τὴν δόξαν chap. 1.14, ὄψῃ τὴν δόξαν chap. 11.40 and εἶδεν τὴν δόξαν chap. 12.41), but there are passages where θεάομαι (chap. 1.38 4.35; 6.5; 11.45) and θεωρεῖν (chap. 6.19; 10.12, etc.) signify without doubt seeing in the flesh.[2] In other passages both meanings are present, and it is typically Johannine that the evangelist should use the verbs in their double meaning.[3]

There is therefore no contradiction in the fact that the necessity of seeing in the flesh is stressed on the one hand and that of faith on the other hand. In actual fact, this method of setting two things side by side is characteristic of all the fourth evangelist's thinking and of the aim which he pursues.

As for the necessity of seeing, we have already quoted the word of the Prologue (which runs parallel to the beginning of the first Epistle of John, where all human faculties are, as

---

[1] See R. Bultmann in *Th. Wb. z. N.T.*, Vol. I, page 711 ff.

[2] See Walter Bauer, *Griechisch-Deutsches Wörterbuch zu den Schriften des Neuen Testaments*, on θεάομαι and θεωρέω.

[3] See O. Cullmann, *Der johanneische Gebrauch doppeldeutiger Ausdrücke als Schlüssel zum Verständnis des vierten Evangeliums (Theol. Zeitschrift, 1948, page 360 ff)* and under page 50 ff.

it were, summoned as witnesses): 'we have *seen* His glory' (ἐθεασάμεθα chap. 1.14). Not only the above mentioned use of the word θεάομαι but also the context (ὁ λόγος σάρξ ἐγένετο) shows that here seeing in the flesh is quite certainly included in the meaning. This assertion is made independently of the question as to the consequences this might have for the problem of authorship, which would demand an examination of the meaning of the first person plural.[1]

In the account of the resurrection of Lazarus the evangelist purposely passes on to us Jesus' expression of joy that the disciples have the opportunity of seeing the miracle, of being present as eyewitnesses: 'And I am glad *for your sakes* that I was not there (at the time of his illness) to the intent ye may believe' (chap. 11.15). Taken together with v. 21: ('if thou hadst been here my brother had not died'), this can only mean that the disciples should have the opportunity of *seeing* the miracle of raising the dead, in order to attain to faith. In fact we hear in v. 45 that 'many of the Jews which came to Mary and had seen (θεασάμενοι) the things which Jesus did, believed on him'.

Similarly Jesus says in chapter 12.30 that the voice from heaven came *for the sake of the crowd that stood by.*

In these passages the main point is that the witnesses really see with their eyes and hear with their ears. We should mention here also the account of the running of the two disciples to Jesus' grave. The beloved disciple, who was first to reach it and go into the grave, sees and believes (chap. 20.8). The following verse underlines, as it were, the necessity of seeing and believing with the thought that the two disciples did not as yet understand the Scriptures as pointing to the fact that he must rise.

We find the same line of thought in Thomas' having to

---

[1] See R. Bultmann, *Das Evangelium des Johannes*, 1941, page 45 f and F. Torm, *Die Psychologie des vierten Evangeliums: Augenzeuge oder nicht?* ZNW, 1931, page 125 ff.

touch the risen Christ before he can believe (chap. 20.27). Indeed Jesus says to him afterwards: 'Because thou hast seen me thou hast believed; blessed are they which have not seen and yet have believed.' In these words here at the end of the Gospel reference is made, as has already been said, to those who no longer have the opportunity of seeing, and the readers of the Gospel are in this situation. These are then addressed directly two verses later and indeed specifically with reference to their faith: ἵνα πιστεύητε (that ye might believe). The Thomas story, therefore, holds, as it were, the key to the Johannine understanding of the whole life of Jesus. But Thomas the apostle himself must see, he must touch. The last words of the risen Christ are not necessarily words of reprimand only, since the other apostles too, mentioned in v. 5.19 ff, had to see Jesus' hands and side.[1] Besides, Thomas did in fact attain to true faith, he makes the best confession of faith the fourth evangelist knows: 'My Lord and my God!' (v. 28).

Here too, however, seeing *alone* is not sufficient to enable one to come to this faith. The eyewitnesses *had* to see, but *for them also* something else had to be added to the seeing. For that reason we have quite a number of passages which stress, in contrast to passages mentioned above, the inadequacy of seeing and set it over against faith. For Thomas (chap. 20.28), as for the beloved disciple (chap. 20.8) seeing had to be followed by faith. The inadequacy of seeing comes more clearly to light, however, in passages where faith did *not* follow. In the above mentioned narrative of the raising of Lazarus, where Jesus expressly emphasizes that the miracle was performed in order that it could be observed by those with him (chap. 11.15), we read that many did in fact believe as a result (chap. 11.45). The evangelist remarks in the following verse, however, v. 46, 'but some of them' went to the Pharisees, to inform them of what had happened, and the note which follows about the

[1] Markus Barth has rightly stressed this in *Der Augenzeuge*, 1946, page 196 f.

consequences of this report shows clearly that these 'some' (τινες) had informed the Pharisees of what had been 'seen' but did so with evil intent, that is in unbelief. Their seeing had not led them to faith.

Various other passages in the Gospel point to the fact that there were many in the lifetime of Jesus who saw the works of Jesus with their eyes, many also who heard his words, but who had not attained the faith which is the necessary accompaniment of having seen and heard. 'Seeing' and 'believing' do not therefore follow one upon the other simply as a matter of course. Already in chapter 2.23 the evangelist remarks that, after the miracle at the marriage in Cana, there were many people in Jerusalem who believed, after they had seen the miracles done by Jesus. *But Jesus did not trust himself unto them*. In other words a faith which is based exclusively on seeing is not sufficient. A faith derived from things seen and nothing more is not true faith.

The evangelist's purpose in making these remarks is to remind his readers that true faith is an act which fulfils itself in the hearts of those who believe. This inner act must be added to seeing and hearing. Thus in chapter 4.48 Jesus at first rebukes the nobleman and with him his whole generation: 'Except ye see signs and wonders, ye will not believe', and the story which follows has all the more point when we learn that the nobleman does then believe, *without seeing* (v. 50), when Jesus says to him: 'Thy son liveth!' Faith comes here not as a result of seeing the miracle, but as a result of an inner attitude of mind which the nobleman adopts toward the 'word' of Jesus.

The familiar synoptic motif, the crowd's longing for miracles, serves also in chapter 6 to establish the inadequacy of merely seeing. When, in v. 30, the Jews ask: 'what sign shewest thou then, that we may see and believe thee?' the πιστεύειν is to be understood as something imperfect, because based on seeing, as in chapter 2.23, without the real inner act of faith, therefore something derived. The Jews have previously seen the miracle of feeding. In fact Jesus must say to them, a few verses further on (v. 36), 'ye also have seen and believe not'.

In chapter 7.5 we hear that even Jesus' brothers did not believe and certainly according to v. 3 they had the opportunity of seeing his 'works'.

Chapter 14.7 ff also speaks of the inadequacy of merely seeing. The statement of Jesus: 'From henceforth ye know the Father, and have seen him', is completely misunderstood by Philip who asks, 'Lord, shew us the Father and it sufficeth us,' and Jesus has to reprimand him, repeating the statement: 'Have I been so long time with you, and dost thou not know me?'

The Thomas story, chapter 20.24 ff, may again be mentioned here. Although, as we have asserted, the actual seeing appears there as a necessity for the apostle living in the lifetime of Jesus, the other idea plays an equally important part, the idea that believing, which must be added to seeing, is more important than seeing. That seeing in the flesh alone is in itself of little account is also expressed in the words in chapter 9.39: 'For judgement I am come into the world, that they which see not might see, and that they which see might be made blind.' βλέπειν (to see) is here used in its double sense.[1]

Again where seeing in the flesh is necessarily presupposed, the second meaning, that of a spiritual seeing, is usually kept in mind alongside as a challenge. This very interplay of 'seeing with the eyes' and 'seeing in faith' is characteristic of our Gospel. That is true of the above mentioned v. 14 of the Prologue and also of chapter 6.40 and 14.19.

It may even be found therefore that as in chapter 11.40, the sequence is reversed: 'If thou wouldest believe, thou shouldest see the glory of God.'[2]

Texts referring to hearing also include often the demand for a more than acoustical hearing. At any rate, in the episode of

[1] Page 53 and page 102 f.   [2] cf. chapter 1.51.

45

the voice from heaven which we mentioned, chapter 12.28 ff, it is assumed that the crowd, for whose benefit the sound was made (v. 30), were meant to perceive in it the glorification of Christ by God, while actually they hear only the noise and say it thundered.

Corresponding to this simultaneous seeing in the flesh and seeing and recognizing in faith there is the double meaning of the word usually used to designate the *object* of seeing and believing. The writer does not use our modern concept of incident, but that of a 'sign' (σημεῖον) and thereby he means to point again to the double quality of an event at once visible and demanding a higher understanding in the context of faith.

* * *

A concept which is strongly stressed by the evangelist is that of the divine *predestination*. It is significant in this connexion that these texts also connect with the understanding in faith of the life of Jesus and are likewise written with the readers' own generation in view. Why was it that some believed and others did not, when they all saw at that time, and why, in the author's own day, do some people believe while others remain impenitent, when both hear the witness to the life of Jesus. The text already mentioned, which speaks of those who do not see, those who see, and those who become blind (chap. 9.39), represents a variation of the synoptic logia (Mark 4.11; Matt. 13.3; Luke 8.10), which are founded on Isaiah 6.9. The evangelist answers much more directly with the Isaiah text in chap. 12.37 ff the question why so many did not believe in Jesus, although he had done so many miracles before them. Throughout the whole Gospel there runs the thought that only those who are 'given' to Christ by the Father, whom the Father 'draws', come to him. That is said with reference to this very subject of believing and seeing in the passage chapter 6.36 ff, 44.65. The Isaiah text about blinding and hardening of the heart is also in the background here.

This line of thought recurs in chapter 8.43 ff with reference to those who cannot hear, and again in chapter 10.25.

* * *

That inner act of faith, we said, was necessary for those who themselves saw the incarnate Logos, before they could really believe what they had beheld. This was all the more necessary for the generation living after Jesus' death and resurrection. But the evangelist goes now a step further. After the resurrection of Christ that act of faith is not only necessary, but *understanding* is *easier* than in Jesus' lifetime. In fact spiritual understanding which is the presupposition of faith but not identical with it, is only possible through the work of the Holy Spirit and this operates only since the glorification of Christ (chap. 7.39). This thought is of the greatest importance for the author. The readers of the Gospel cannot say therefore that they are in a less favourable situation than those who saw Christ in the flesh. On the contrary they are to some extent in a preferable position to those who lived *only* in the time of the incarnate Christ. They have now the Holy Spirit and he opens their understanding in faith and reveals to them the deeper meaning of the events of Jesus' life. On the other hand these events are reported to them as material facts through the eyewitness of the apostles and these can serve as a buttress for their faith (chap. 17.20). This foundation is for them also quite indispensable but the true understanding is only possible since the time when Christ 'was glorified', i.e. since he sent the Paraclete, the Spirit of truth.

Even eye and ear witness can reach complete understanding and full comprehension of its deeper meaning only after Jesus' death and resurrection. We have seen that some did actually attain to faith in Jesus' lifetime. They too, however, can grasp the deeper significance of his life, its connexion, in the history of salvation, with past and present, only after the glorification of Christ. All the sayings which the author reproduces in the

47

farewell discourses, chapters 14-16, have therefore for him as an evangelist an intensely personal value. They justify to some extent his whole literary undertaking; the Holy Spirit which Jesus promised in that hour on the eve of his death has invested him, the evangelist also, with the special understanding of Jesus' life, which he in his work communicates to his readers.

But now, if those who *saw* the events required to have a higher knowledge, which has only become possible since Christ's glorification, the readers' own generation needs all the more the help of the Spirit of truth. He was promised them by Christ and is at work in the faithful, meeting this need, i.e., with special reference to the *understanding of the earthly life of Jesus*. Thus the two passages of the farewell address, chapter 14.26 and 16.12, provide, so to speak, the key to the understanding of our Gospel. 'The Holy Ghost, whom the Father will send in my name, he shall teach you all things and bring all things to your *remembrance*, whatsoever I have said unto you.' (chap. 14.26.) 'I have yet many things to say unto you, but ye cannot bear them now. Howbeit when he, the Spirit of truth is come, he will guide you into all truth.' (chap. 16.12 ff.)

It has not been sufficiently observed that the efficacy of the Paraclete applies, in the first instance, to the *understanding of the life of Jesus*. There is a great deal of talk about the self-consciousness of Jesus. In thinking about John's Gospel we should also speak of the self-consciousness of the evangelist, of his consciousness of being inspired by the Paraclete. In this consciousness he has written an account of the events of Jesus' life in that particular perspective which distinguishes this Gospel from the others.

In the course of his narrative, therefore, the writer is constantly impressing on his readers that those who have seen all these events have grasped their true meaning only *after* Jesus' death and resurrection. At the end of the account of the clearing of the Temple, chapter 2.19, he writes expressly that *after* the death of the Lord the disciples '*remembered*' that he had told them about his body, which must be destroyed. All passages in the Fourth Gospel which speak of this 'remembering'[1] belong to the same category as the pronouncements about the Paraclete in the farewell discourses and have a far greater importance for the understanding of what is peculiarly Johannine than is immediately apparent. This 'remembering' is not merely a remembering of the material facts, it includes alongside of this that understanding of the facts which is first granted through the Holy Spirit. Thanks to this special remembering in the Holy Spirit the evangelist also understands for the first time the connexion in the history of salvation of the life of Jesus with the Old Testament. When, in the course of his narrative, he points to this connexion, he remarks expressly that the eyewitnesses realized this only later.

In chapter 12.16, therefore, he mentions that the fact that Jesus sat on an ass is a fulfilment of Isaiah 40.9 and Zech. 9.9 and intentionally adds here too: 'These things understood not the disciples at the first: but when Jesus was glorified, then *remembered* they that these things were written of him and that they had done these things unto him.' Jesus' words to Peter, spoken when he is washing his feet, also belong here: 'What I do thou knowest not now, but thou shalt know hereafter.' (chap. 13.7.) In this text, as we shall see,[2] it is a question of understanding the connexion of what happened at that time with the community's present. On the other hand the already mentioned remark of the evangelist in chapter 20.9 refers indirectly to the likewise later recognition (οὐδέπω, not yet) of the Old Testament witness for Christ's resurrection. The author's postscripts in chapter 12.32 and chapter 18.32 also depend on a deeper understanding of a word of Jesus—the understanding which revealed to the evangelist only later his connexion with the past and the future of the history of salvation.

---

[1] See N. A. Dahl, *Anamnesis. Mémoire et commémoration dans le christianisme primitif (Studia theologica,* 1947) page 94.   [2] Page 105.

When we have regard to all these references where the evangelist makes known to us his literary personality and purpose, we see that it must be the *task of the exegete* of this Gospel to allow for this purpose in all its parts. It will not be sufficient, therefore, to treat a reported fact only in material terms, we shall have to ask what are its connexions with the whole history of salvation which have been made accessible to the evangelist in virtue of that 'remembering' in the Spirit, and because of which he has chosen these particular facts. More than that, we shall have to pursue these connexions, determined by his selection, *in places where he has not made them particularly explicit but has only hinted at them,*[1] for he trusts in the capacity for understanding which the Paraclete affords the readers also. They should share that ability of the evangelist to understand the once-for-all historical event or the once spoken word of Jesus comprehensively, so to speak, in their soteriological context and development.

* * *

We shall now show further by a linguistic proof that this twofold understanding is plainly the Johannine intention, and that it belongs to the programme of the Gospel. Our linguistic proof will depend on the extraordinarily frequent use of double or ambiguous expressions,[2] which use has been repeatedly affirmed in previous paragraphs in the present work.[3]

The third chapter furnishes us with several examples of this Johannine use of words with two meanings which must both be expressed together. First of all we must mention the adverb

---

[1] For the *necessity* of reckoning with more passing references see page 52 and page 68, note 2.

[2] See above page 41, K. L. Schmidt. The Johannine character of the narrative of the Miracle at the Marriage Feast at Cana in Galilee in Harnack-Ehrung, 1921, has already referred to this peculiarity, especially with reference to the use of the word πόθεν (p. 41).

[3] In what follows I give a resumé of my more detailed article on this question, *Der johanneische Gebrauch doppeldeutiger Ausdrucke als Schlüssel zum Verständnis des vierten Evangeliums (Theologische Zeitschrift,* 1948, p. 360 ff).

ἄνωθεν (from above) joined with the verb γεννηθῆναι.
Already in ancient times, the exegetes of John's Gospel discussed the question whether here we have the chronological
use of the word, 'anew', or the local use 'from above'. It is,
however, characteristic of our Gospel that here there is no
question of an alternative, rather both are meant. Nicodemus'
clumsy misunderstanding, as if it was a question of a birth ἐκ
τῆς κοιλίας τῆς μητρός (from his mother's womb) concerns
only the verb γεννηθῆναι (to be born), not the interpretation
of the ἄνωθεν in the sense of δεύτερον. For, according to
the evangelist, Jesus also means a real second birth (v. 7).
There can be no doubt, however, that ἄνωθεν here, as in 3.31
and 19.11, means also and at the same time 'from above', and
Nicodemus has not realized this. We shall see[1] how, with this
reference to the local sense, the following verses (12 ff) exhibit
the christological foundation of the 'new' birth: 'No man hath
ascended into heaven but he that descended out of heaven,
even the Son of Man.'

The ambiguous word ὑψωθῆναι in this same conversation
with Nicodemus, which follows immediately on the reference
to Christ's ascension (v. 13), is even more important for our
enquiry. This verb has first of all the simple meaning 'lifted
up', when John is talking about the serpent, which Moses
'lifted up' (v. 14). This sense is now extended further to cover
the lifting up of Christ on the Cross. This is no hypothesis,
but is plainly expressed by the evangelist in 12.32 ff: 'And I,
if I be lifted up from the earth, will draw all men unto myself.
But this he said signifying (σημαίνων) *by what manner of death he
should die.*' The connexion shows at the same time, however,
(in 3.14 and 12,32, as also in the further passage 8.28, where
we find the same verb), that the lifting up refers also to the
ascension, in accordance with normal New Testament usage
(Acts 2.33; 5.3; Phil. 2.9). It is interesting that here we have
as it were, a three-cornered reference; the serpent lifted up on

. [1] See under p. 77 f.

high, the One lifted up on high on the Cross, the Son of Man lifted up to heaven. If we did not have, besides the Nicodemus pericope, the above mentioned explanation (12.32) introduced by the evangelist himself, the allusion (chap. 3) to the Cross would be rejected as an unjustified 'allegorical' explanation. This very example confirms, however, that *even in passages where the writer does not expressly say so, as in 3.14, there are references present to further acts of Christ in the history of salvation.*

This same chapter 3 probably contains another word with a double meaning in the much quoted v. 16. The verb ἔδωκεν (gave) may be used here first in the sense of ἀπέστειλεν (sent) (1 John 4.9): God has sent his Son into the world. At this point, however, where we have established a reference to the Cross, there is present almost certainly at the same time the sense of παρέδωκεν (Rom. 8.32): He hath 'delivered him up' to death. Thus the words of double meaning accumulate in this chapter in a manner particularly suited to sharpen our watch for this Johannine peculiarity, and we shall try now to mention the remaining most important examples, in order of chapters. The entire number of them would be far greater than that given here.[1]

In 1.37 ff, which deals with the first meeting with disciples, the evangelist uses the verb ἀκολουθεῖν first of all literally, in vv. 37 and 38. The two disciples follow after Jesus so that he has to turn around in order to look at them. On the other hand in vv. 40 and 44 it is clear that this word signifies at the same time continuous following in discipleship. The word occurs again in a similar double sense in the dialogue between Jesus and Peter in 13.36 ff.

The examination of the use of the verb ὑψόω (raise) in 3.14 showed that this same word could be used in more than two connexions, and we shall make the same claim for the 'bread of life' and the 'water of life'. The ὕδωρ ζῶν in chapter 4.10 signifies first of all running water in contrast to stagnant water.

---

[1] See O. Cullmann's article mentioned above, p. 50, note 3.

In the second place, there is present the general sense 'well of life', corresponding to the Hebraic figurative use of מים חיים an attribute of Jahweh in the Old Testament. According to 7.39, however, the fourth evangelist understands under ὕδωρ ζῶν thirdly, and more precisely, the Holy Spirit, and we shall seek to indicate further, here, as in 3.5, a connexion with the water of Baptism. In this case we find as many as four meanings for the same word!

Very much the same is true of the parallel expression ἄρτος τῆς ζωῆς (6.35, 48). Here, too, we start with material bread, given to satisfy the crowd in the miracle. From there the line runs to that other bread which in the Old Testament was given by God, in a likewise miraculous fashion, as ἄρτος ἐκ τοῦ οὐρανοῦ (bread from heaven), Manna. This is then further connected simultaneously with the Person of Christ and the eucharistic bread of the early Church. This word, with its varied reference within the history of salvation, reminds us in form of ὑψόω in 3.14 and in content especially of ὕδωρ ζῶν.

The story of the healing of the man blind from birth hinges on the words of Jesus about the τυφλοί (9.39 ff), which we have already mentioned, and it is quite clear that in view of the double usage of the word 'blind', already current in Judaism, the word here means at once physically and spiritually blind. Similarly in the story of the wonderful healing of the lame man of Bethesda in 5.6 ff the adjective ὑγιής is used for physically healthy. From the remarks of Jesus in 7.23, however, which have this healing in view and which set it expressly parallel to circumcision, it is evident that, in using this word, Jesus had, at the same time, at the back of his mind the thought of religious and ethical purity.

The words concerning resurrection in the Lazarus story (11.24 ff) form the centre of the whole Gospel and it is significant for our thesis that in this important passage the verb ἀναστῆναι is used both in the current sense of the resurrection at the last day and in the sense of an anticipation of the resurrection possible now in the present, a sense conceivable for the author in the light of the glorification of Christ. 'Thy brother shall rise again,' says Jesus to Martha (v. 24). She thinks he is speaking of the resurrection at the last day, and certainly this direct meaning of the word should not be excluded here, for faith in the future resurrection at the end of the age is clearly attested in John's Gospel (6.39, 40, 44, 54; and 5.29), and it will not do to cut out all these passages with R. Bultmann as interpolations. There is no trace of the modern antithesis of present 'mystical' and future eschatological events in John's gospel. There is no question here of an alternative, but rather of the Christ events interpenetrating the history of salvation. Thus it is very important for the evangelist that Jesus speaks against the background of the faith in the resurrection at the last day shared by him with Judaism. This resurrection is in Christ who is himself 'the resurrection and the life' and it is already there for all who believe in him (v. 25). The evangelist subsequently finds that a sign of this explanation of the resurrection is already given in the rising of Lazarus, which was certainly regarded by him as historical event. Here is a third type of resurrection. It, too, is not final resurrection, as at the last day, for Lazarus will have to die again after the resurrection recounted in the narrative. Nor can it be put simply in the category of the post-Paschal present resurrection of all faithful, of which we have spoken. Rather it points to both; on the one hand to the final resurrection, on the other hand—*and here is the main point*—to the anticipation which after Easter is reality for *all* faithful. Here in the person of Lazarus, Christ has given during his earthly ministry *a sign* before Easter, which points forward to the fact that later, whosoever believes on Christ 'though he die, yet shall he live, and whosoever liveth and believeth on me shall never die'. This saying too, which brings out clearly the present reference of the event, is based on the double sense of the two verbs ζῆν and ἀποθνήσκειν; they are used interchangeably in their physical and theological sense.[1]

The familiar word on the Cross τετέλεσται (it is finished) in 19.30 (cf. also v. 28) has long been the object of discussion whether it is to be conceived purely chronologically or theologically. But here too it is false to posit an alternative. For in line with the double meaning shared by the noun τέλος in chapter 13.1, the word in John's understanding means certainly both together. 'The life of the incarnate Christ is at an end' and 'his work is fulfilled'.

Besides these words with double meaning we should also mention whole sentences which as such are to be understood in two ways. Among these is the high priest Caiaphas' utterance in 11.50: 'It is expedient for you that one man should die for the people, and that the whole nation perish not.' Only after the death and resurrection of Christ did it strike the evangelist that here there was a theological idea extending beyond the purely historical range of the sentence—the thought of the vicarious suffering,—so that the High Priest, without himself knowing it, had made a pronouncement that was doubly valid. Thus from the smallest literary unit to the greater sentence, from the sentence to the paragraph, from the paragraph to the whole Gospel, we can see how the evangelist

---

[1] This also sheds light on the use of another word in this chapter which has a double meaning, the verb κοιμᾶσθαι in v. 11. The situation here, however, is rather different from that in other passages we have studied. Whereas in these other instances the more abstruse, derived meaning was usually intended, here it is the straightforward meaning that is intended, that of 'sleeping' the last sleep. This, however, presupposes the higher understanding and is appreciated only by the disciples, not by the others present. Of course we may take the other meaning of the verb, quite literally, 'to die'. But although Lazarus is physically dead, yet he is only asleep, since his death is only for a little. Thus his resurrection is an illustration of the fact that, wherever Christ is at work, all 'death' is only a 'sleep'. The matter is therefore rather more complicated here than in the other examples, in so far as the straightforward meaning 'sleep' can be understood with all its theological content only when it is recognized that Jesus, in using the expression κεκοίμηται meant also and indeed first physical death. A higher understanding alone makes it possible to appreciate that of which the Lazarus miracle is meant to be a sign.

endeavours to discover in the once-for-all, thoroughly real, historical events of the life of Christ the further implications for the history of salvation already contained therein as signs, and to awaken in his readers an understanding of this comprehensive perspective for past, present and future.[1]

From various points of view then, we have come to the same conclusion. *The implicit assumption of this Gospel is that the historical events, as here presented, contain in themselves, besides what is immediately perceptible, references to further facts of salvation with which these once-for-all key events are bound up.* 'Historical' and 'symbolic' explanation of the Johannine narratives is therefore a false antithesis. A false alternative is set up, as if, in the evangelist's view, a saying could be meant either *only* as historical fact or *only* as reference to a theological 'mystical' fact. In that way the understanding of this Gospel is obstructed from the start. The evangelist's whole purpose is to present both once-for-all history and the reference of this history to its previous and subsequent course, in one comprehensive perspective.

History is here, therefore, on the one hand, not merely a 'mythological' garment, which one can strip off in order to 'demythologize' the Gospel. But on the other hand, we stress again, in view of the subsequent chapters and of possible objections that it does not mean a lapse into allegorical inter-

---

[1] In the light of the evangelist's deliberate use of words of two meanings, which we have shown, works such as C. F. Burney's *The Aramaic Origin of the Fourth Gospel*, 1922, and Ch.-C Torrey, 'The Aramaic Origin of the Gospel of John' (*Harvard Theological Review*, 1923, p. 305 ff) and J. de Zwaan, 'John wrote in Aramaic' (*Journal of Biblical Literature*, 1938, p. 155 ff) according to which John's Gospel presupposes an Aramaic original, would have to be examined. Their thesis would only hold if it could be shown that the Greek words of double meaning correspond to Aramaic equivalents. Here, however, note that something much more important is to be taken into account if we work from an Aramaic original, besides the Johannine expressions with double meaning which we have collected here. It appears that the Aramaic translation of the words ὁ ἀμνὸς τοῦ θεοῦ ὁ αἴρων τὴν ἁμαρτίαν τοῦ κόσμου means both: 'the Lamb of God that *taketh away* the sin of the world' and 'the *servant* of Jahweh, that *beareth* the sin of the world'. Here the double meaning of the Aramaic words is not reproduced in the Greek.

pretation when one seeks to point out in individual instances
how the author shows, from the different events of Jesus' life,
the identity of the incarnate with the glorified Christ, present,
for example, in the sacraments. Improper allegorizing would
occur only if an appreciation of the historical events were
disputed or the events given a merely pictorial significance.
This is not the case, however, in the present method of enquiry.
On the other hand the search for a meaning going beyond the
once-for-all event would have to be rejected as 'allegorical'
error if it was a case of a document which was obviously concerned to present *only* an historical fact. We have seen, however, that the Gospel of John indicates in so many places the
necessity of a double meaning, that enquiry into the deeper
unexpressed sense is to be raised, in this Gospel, to the status
of a principle of interpretation.

The deeper understanding, of which we speak, refers to
the connexion between the historical life of Jesus and the
entire history of salvation. That implies that it would be false
to think the line runs only to one single point in these events.
It is rather so; some passages point to happenings before the
incarnation of Jesus, others to what happens in the community
of the evangelist's day. We have seen that it sometimes happens
that several references are contained in one and the same passage. If in the following chapters we show a special interest
in the service of worship of the time, an interest which befits
this study, and which finds material in many passages, we are
certainly not saying that the evangelist had only this one
reference in mind, but rather that *other works like this ought to
be written on other contacts of the life of Jesus with the history of
salvation.* I am thinking of the connexion with the Old Testament (which comes, of course, into John's category—
'subsequent remembrance') or of the connexion of the life
of Jesus with the heresies current in the evangelist's time,
docetic heresies and particularly those dealing with John the
Baptist.

We have seen that our evangelist's representation of the life of Jesus is always based on a conspectus of the historical Jesus and the Lord present in the community. The presence of Christ among his people is actualized in the service of worship. This is always represented however, as we saw in a previous chapter on the basic characteristics of the early Christian service of worship, either as Lord's Supper or as Baptism. We have established that, at least as a rule, there is no other setting for the various elements of the service. We shall find an indirect confirmation of this in John's Gospel, which treats the two sacraments as expressions of the whole worship life of the early community and correspondingly sets forth the relation between the Lord of the community *present especially in these two sacraments* and the life of Jesus.

Since in the present work, as already remarked, no thorough-going exegesis of the passages in question can be expected, we must presuppose in many cases the explanation of the facts as such. We want here to show only the interest in the service of worship, for the sake of which the individual facts are related by the evangelist. We must, of course, proceed from the results of exegesis.

The method of enquiry here represented appears to me to show that we can follow a line through the main narratives of the Gospel and need not be content with references appearing intermittently. This, however, is in direct opposition to the most recent commentary on John's Gospel, that of Rudolph Bultmann,[1] who disputes the connexion with Baptism and

[1] R. Bultmann, *Das Evangelium des Johannes*, 1941 (*Kritisch-exegetischer Kommentar über das Neue Testament begr. von* H. A. W. Meyer). A new edition will soon appear.

It is extremely worth while to work through thoroughly the whole volume of literature old and new which, based on this commentary, has long formed an indispensable reference book for John's Gospel.

It is also worth the effort to try really to understand the theological content of all the narratives, though many question marks may have to be appended.

The rearranging of chapters and verses is not intelligible enough to justify its being introduced as a principle for the text to be commented on, in a commentary as objective as that of Meyer. 'Reference' is at all events made extremely difficult.

Lord's Supper, even in passages where their presence was formerly acknowledged by the majority of exegetes. This is not surprising, since Bultmann sees far too exclusively only one line of thought in John's Gospel—revelation through the Word.[1]

On the other hand, the exegesis of the ancient Church recognizes to a considerable degree our Gospel's interest in the liturgy, and the Church Fathers and early Christian art also bear witness to it.[2] In this latter, not only are individual scenes from our Gospel used as illustrations of the sacraments, but throughout the middle ages the tradition persisted of representing John the evangelist himself with the communion cup.

2. JOHN THE BAPTIST AND THE BAPTISM OF JESUS
Chapters 1.6-8; 15.19-34.

In all four Gospels John the Baptist stands at the beginning. In the Fourth Gospel the limitation of his baptizing over against that of Christ is stressed as early as the Prologue, then in his answer to the Jewish delegation and his second witness which is included in it, and again later in chapter 3.22-36 in his last witness—and stressed in a way which shows clearly that here we have a matter of particular concern for the evangelist. From John's baptizing and from Christ's being baptized a line

---

[1] His remarks on p. 360 are particularly characteristic of his rejection of any interest in the sacraments in the Gospel of John. It should however be noted from the beginning that he finds himself compelled, as we shall see, to regard certain *critical* passages as later interpolations—Chapter 3.5; 6.52*b*-58, 19.34*b*-35—in order to maintain his assertion of the evangelist's negative attitude to the sacraments.

[2] Amongst recent students of the question C. T. Craig has made a considerable contribution by pointing out the evangelist's interest in the sacraments in several passages in his treatise 'Sacramental Interest in the Fourth Gospel' (*Journal of Biblical Literature*, 1939, p. 31 ff).

W. H. Raney, *The Relation of the Fourth Gospel to the Christian Cultus*, 1933, even attempts to prove, by means of a comparison with the rhythm of semitic hymns that the Prologue, the Johannine discourses, and other pieces represent in form 'prose hymns' which were meant to be sung by a choir as prelude or postlude to the public reading of the narrative parts in the service.

should be drawn to the Baptism which Christ brought and which is practised in the early Christian community. The evangelist's interest in the present is here already apparent in a presentation of the events which diverges characteristically from that of the synoptics. If we had nothing besides these Baptism passages, their connexion with Christian Baptism might appear problematic. But as it is we shall affirm throughout the whole of John's Gospel an extraordinary interest in 'water', and it is in this connexion that these Johannine introductory passages must be read.

According to chapter 1.19-28 a deputation of priests and Levites was sent to the Baptist. In the composition of the delegation, the context of public worship of the passage is immediately evident. The delegation is composed of men who specialize in questions of liturgical propriety. The Baptist himself tells later what happened at the Baptism of Jesus and from that point on he designates Jesus as 'Lamb of God that taketh away the sins of the world'. This, as we shall see, effects the transition to the positive significance of Christian Baptism. The hypothesis that the evangelist sees in Jesus' being baptized a pointer to the Baptism of the Christian community means just this—that he rightly understood the significance of Jesus' Baptism, since it is in fact the historical origin of Christian Baptism.[1] First of all, however, we must define this Baptism of Christ.

Even the Prologue shows that all John's baptizing is to be regarded not as of importance in itself, but only *as pointer* to Christ. In the author's day there were people who ascribed to John's baptism a value quite independent of Christ—the Baptist's disciples, who claimed, after their master's death, that John the Baptist himself was the Christ, although John had never made this claim in his lifetime. In the Jewish-Christian Pseudo-Clementine writings[2] we hear that the mem-

---

[1] cf. W. F. Flemington, *The New Testament Doctrine of Baptism*, 1948, p. 29 ff.
[2] Rec I, 54, 60.

bers of this sect actually taught that John the Baptist was the Messiah. Perhaps the people whom we meet in Ephesus in Acts 19.3 and of whom it is said, they had known only the baptism of John, belong here also. We know further that in the writings of the Mandeans, whose religious system certainly represents a late syncretic product, which stands nevertheless in some relation at an early stage to the sect of the disciples of John, John appears as the antagonist of Jesus, who is designated the false Messiah.[1] Primitive Christianity had evidently to combat such people from earliest times, especially in Syria, where Gnostic tendencies became attached to the claim of John's disciples. We ascertain this in the Pseudo-Clementine Jewish-Christian source, the Κηρύγματα Πέτρου (Gospel of Peter). In the so-called Syzygian canon the divine action is schematized in successive pairs, of which the left is the evil principle or false prophecy and the right the good principle or true prophecy. It is noteworthy that John the Baptist figures among the representatives of false prophecy.[2] That is the outcome of a controversy which evidently existed between Jewish Christians and sects following John. This polemic obviously shoots beyond the mark here in so far as John the Baptist himself is not to be made responsible for the false evaluation of his person made by his followers.

The Gospel of John, which was concerned to combat that false conception of the rôle of the Baptist, did not fall into the error of the Jewish Christians. It does, however, stress with particular emphasis that this false estimation is entirely contrary to the Baptist's own intention. For this reason, in this Gospel, even in the account of the Baptism of Jesus it is not the author himself who speaks, as in the synoptics, but he allows the Baptist to speak. As early as the Prologue every-

---

[1] See R. Bultmann, *Die Bedeutung der neuerschlossenen mandäischen und manichäischen Quellen für das Verständnis des Johannes-Evangeliums* in *ZNW*, 1925, p. 100 ff.

[2] Ps. Clem. *Hom.* II, 17. Sufficient notice is not taken of this passage. cf O. Cullmann. *Le problème littéraire et historique du roman pseudoclémentin*, 1930, p. 89 and 240 ff.

thing is directed towards the Baptist's purpose of witness.[1] Already here where we read of the eternal Logos, the true light, John the Baptist appears, and of him it is said significantly, he is *not* the light. Rather he is brought in only as witness. Even the apparent privilege of chronological priority on which the disciples of John loved to dwell, even that was emphatically rejected by the Baptist himself at the end of the Prologue. 'He that cometh after me is become before me' (vv. 15 and 30).[2]

The Baptist's witness contained in the passage about the Jewish delegation dismisses most strongly[3] that false estimation. The evangelist cannot find words enough to hammer into his readers that the historical John the Baptist wanted nothing to do with fulfilling his mission independently of him that should 'come after him': 'and he confessed and denied not, and he confessed.'[4] We see here how, in John's Gospel, the line is traced back from the author's present, from the present of the early community to the time of Jesus' incarnation. It is already a question of Baptism and more specifically it is a question of a *rejection of a continuance of the baptism of John* after Christ has introduced Baptism by the Spirit. This continuance is opposed by the Baptist himself in his own words. Where Christ is present, there is no more preparatory Baptism.

The witness of the Baptist contains also the *positive*

---

[1] W. Baldensperger has shown this very clearly in *Der Prolog des vierten Evangeliums*, 1898.

[2] It is interesting that the pseudo-Clementine Κηρύγματα Πέτρου also turn this chronological argument against John. In the Syzygian canon already mentioned (p. 61), the following principle operates from Adam on: within each pair that one who comes first represents always false prophecy; that one who comes second the true: so Cain before Abel, Ishmael before Isaac, Esau before Jacob, Paul before Peter, Antichrist before Christ. So too John the Baptist, the forerunner (πρόοδος *Hom.* II, 23) before the Son of Man (see also *Hom.* II, 17) cf. O. Cullmann, *Le problème littéraire et historique du roman pseudoclémentin*, p. 240 f and 'Ο ὀπίσω μου ἐρχόμενος in *Coniectanea Neotestamentica in honorem A. Fridrichsen*, 1947, p. 26 ff.

[3] ὡμολόγησεν καὶ οὐκ ἠρνήσατο καὶ ὡμολόγησεν ὅτι ἐγὼ οὐκ εἰμὶ ὁ Χριστός

[4] The Baptist himself rejects here (v. 21) even the honour of being Elias, the Prophet (who should come at the end), the title given him by Jesus in the synoptics (Matt. 11.14; 17.10-13).

reference to Christian Baptism, whose essential character exists in the fact that to the water the *Spirit* is added. The Baptist clothes this reference in the narrative which runs from v. 29 in the form of an account of the Baptism of Jesus. But first of all the Baptist answers the Jewish delegates' question (v. 28) why he *baptizes* when he is not the Messiah and not Elias and not the Prophet in v. 26: 'I baptize with water, in the midst of you standeth even he that cometh after me. . . .' He does not yet say here: who will baptize you with the Spirit, as in the second witness in v. 33 and as in Mark (1.8), but, in contrast to his water baptism, he simply mentions here the fact that the person of the Other is there. It is the person of Jesus, not the baptizing, that is first set over against the baptizing of John. The thought at first implicit, is this, that the significance of all Baptism is achieved in *the person* of Jesus himself. Already here—if we are right in believing that the evangelist has his eye on the present in this whole passage—it is indicated that Christian Baptism is wholly bound up with the person of Christ. For this reason it is Baptism with the Spirit. Christ first instituted true Baptism, as we see now in the following verses, in that he himself was baptized in his death—when he sacrificed his life for the sins of others.

We see here in the account of Jesus' own Baptism how closely Christian Baptism is connected with the *Death of Christ*, in the designation of Jesus by the Baptist (v. 29): 'Behold the Lamb of God, which taketh away the sin of the world.' Note that the evangelist makes this story follow the account of the Jewish delegation to the Baptist, and it will not do to explain this from the synoptic arrangement of material. He must rather have seen an inner connexion between the two. That connexion can only lie in the fact that the Baptist's activity, i.e. his water baptism, is confronted with the Baptism of Jesus, here interpreted as Baptism in death, and confronted in such a way that on both occasions the Baptist himself figures as witness. Even the synoptic record of the Baptism of Jesus has the deeper sense that in his Baptism it falls to Jesus to undertake the rôle of the servant of God, suffering vicariously for his people, for the voice from heaven repeats a word which in Isaiah 42.1 is directed to the Suffering Servant, the Ebed Jahweh.[1] This connexion with Isaiah 42.1 is still clearer in John's Gospel, for here in v. 34, at least according to the reading of the Sinaitic, old Latin and old Syriac translation, the word is quoted more precisely: 'This is the ἐκλεκτός (chosen) of God.' According to the Septuagint translation, the Ebed Jahweh is referred to in this verse.[2] While all other Jews submit themselves to John's baptism only for their own sins, Christ must undergo as it were a general Baptism, fulfilling the mission of the Suffering Servant, a Baptism which is for the benefit of all and which therefore makes the baptism of John superfluous.

In John's Gospel this thought stands out in bold relief in that Christ's designation ἀμνὸς τοῦ Θεοῦ ὁ αἴρων τὴν ἁμαρτίαν τοῦ κόσμου twice appears as the centre and climax of the Baptist's witness, in v. 29 before the account of the Baptism of Jesus and immediately afterwards in v. 36, where, following on this testimony, two men formerly disciples of John become disciples of Jesus. We have to admit that in the Greek, in the expression 'Lamb of God, that taketh away the sin of the world', it appears that the writer has in mind the sacrificial lamb which *bears away* sin (αἴρειν) rather than the Suffering Servant who bears it (φέρειν). But surely it is a question there of related thoughts.[3] Besides we have to

[1] See O. Cullmann, 'La signification du baptême dans le Nouveau Testament' in *Revue de Theologie et de Philosophie* (Lausanne) 1942, p. 121 ff and *Die Tauflehre des Neuen Testaments*, 1948, p. 5 ff. See especially p. 15 f.

[2] ἐκλεκτός is a translation of the Hebrew *bechiri*. The reading υἱός represents a later harmonizing of the Johannine text with the text of the synoptics. A. Harnack, *Studien zur Geschichte des N.T.s* and *der alter Kirche*, 1931, p. 127 ff and A. Loisy, *Le quatrième Evangile*, 2nd ed., 1921, also adopt the reading ἐκλεκτός as original.

[3] See especially Strack-Billerbeck, *Kommentar z. N.T. aus Talmud und Midrasch*, Vol. II, p. 367 ff.

remember that in Isaiah 53.7 the Servant of God is *compared* to a lamb; 'as a lamb that is led to the slaughter. . . . ' Lastly it is worthy of careful note that the Aramaic word for 'lamb' טליא has at the same time the meaning 'servant'. If, as Schlatter has already tried to prove[1] and C. F. Burney[2] probably has done in a painstaking investigation, if I say, the mother tongue of the author of John's Gospel was really Aramaic, then we have a further proof that by 'Lamb of God'[3] the Ebed Jahweh is meant, to whom at the Baptism the voice from heaven refers.[4] The Aramaic verb נטל also which, according to Strack-Billerbeck,[5] is used as an equivalent for αἴρειν fits just as well the sacrificial lamb, which 'removes' sin as the Suffering Servant who 'bears' it.[6]

Thus there stands right at the beginning of John's Gospel the reference to the *institution* of *Christian Baptism* by him who as 'Lamb' has removed the sin of the world and has therefore fulfilled the meaning of all Baptism and brought Baptism with the Spirit. The Baptist beheld the Spirit 'descend and abide upon him' (v. 32). John's Gospel alone stresses that the Spirit 'abode' on Jesus ἔμεινε. It is important for the Fourth Gospel that it was not a question of a mere momentary manifestation of the Spirit, but that the Spirit took possession[7] of him, who from now on brings Baptism with the Spirit.

[1] A. Schlatter, *Sprache und Heimat des vierten Evangelisten*, 1902.

[2] C. F. Burney, *The Aramaic Origin of the Fourth Gospel*, 1922.

[3] The genitive τοῦ Θεοῦ suits Ebed Jahweh much more than sacrificial Lamb.

[4] E. Lohmeyer, also, *Die Offenbarung des Johannes* (*Hdb. z. N.T.*) 1926, is inclined with Burney to regard ἀρνίον as the translation of the Aramaic טליא. Bultmann's view, *op. cit.*, p. 47, that the Aramaic N.T. עבדא would have been nearer is not convincing.

[5] *Kommentar zu N.T. aus Talmud und Midrasch*, Vol. II, p. 370.

[6] The Greek verb αἴρειν can moreover sometimes have the meaning φέρειν; in John's Gospel, however, it means 'take away'; in the LXX we find at Isa. 53.4, 11, 12 not αἴρειν but (ἀνα)φέρειν. J. Jeremias in *Th. Wb. z. N.T.*, Vol. I, p. 343 is also inclined to identify from the evangelist's translation ἀμνός, the *original* connexion with the servant of God, Aramaic טליא. See also his article "Ἀμνός τοῦ Θεοῦ—παῖς Θεοῦ" *Zeitschr. für die N.T. Wissenschaft*, 1935, p. 115.

[7] Note that the verse quoted (Isaiah 42.1 God speaking) goes on 'I have put my spirit upon him' (the servant of Jahweh).

John's Gospel thus indirectly bears witness to the conception of Christian Baptism as a Baptism into the death of Christ corresponding to the Pauline teaching in Romans 6 and the meaning which the verb 'be baptized' had for Jesus even in the synoptic Logia, when he speaks of his Baptism: *viz.* 'to die' (Mark 10.39: Luke 13.50). The sacrament of Baptism points us to the death of Christ; that is a thought which we shall come across again in John's Gospel. But first there follows in chapter 2 a passage in which the Lord's Supper on its side is placed in relationship to the death of Christ. As Christian Baptism is defined over against the Baptism of John, so the Lord's Supper is defined over against Jewish 'purification'.

3. THE MARRIAGE AT CANA Chapter 2.1-11

It belongs to the nature of the Johannine 'miracle', the σημεῖον, that in a particular way the plain historical fact contains a reference to the Christ event which continues in the community of the Church.

Here we must start from the answer which Jesus gives in v. 4: '*Mine hour is not yet come.*' What sort of hour is meant here? It is obviously not the hour of the changing of earthly water into earthly wine, since that hour is indeed come. It is noteworthy that this text about the coming of the hour occurs at several points in John's Gospel and not only here. First, chapter 7.30: 'the Jews sought to take him, and no man laid his hand on him, because *his hour was not yet come.*' The hour here meant is obviously the hour of Jesus' death. Then chapter 8.20: 'These words spake he as he taught in the temple: and no man took him; because *his hour was not yet come.*' Here too it is clear that the hour which is not yet come is the hour of Jesus' death. Again chapter 12.23: 'Jesus answereth them saying: 'The hour is come that the Son of man should be glorified.' The glorification of Jesus coincides in John's Gospel with his death. Further chapter 13.1: 'Now before the feast of the passover, Jesus knowing that *his hour was come* that he should depart out of this world unto the Father. . . . ' Again it is the hour of his death which is in question. Finally chapter 17.1 at the beginning of the high priestly prayer: 'Father, *the hour is come*! Glorify thy Son.' There can be no doubt that here, too, the hour of his death is meant.

We have still the following passage to add, which confirms our findings, chapter 7.1-10. This passage contains in v. 6 the sentence: '*My time is not yet come.*' Although καιρός not ὤρα is the word here used, the sense is the same. The time is the time for 'going up to Jerusalem to the Feast' and Jesus is thinking of the time when, for the last time, he will go up to Jerusalem to supper. The passage is important as providing an analogy to the Cana story. In the one it is his mother who urges Jesus to proclaim his Messianic glory by performing a miracle, in the other in chapter 7.1 ff, it is the brothers of Jesus, i.e. also representatives of his family who exhort him to get away to Jerusalem in order openly to manifest his glory by his works. In the Cana story Jesus declines to do his mother's bidding and offers as reason: 'My hour is not yet come.' Likewise he declines to carry out his brother's advice in chapter 7 and gives as the reason for his refusal: 'I go not up yet unto this feast: because My time is not yet fulfilled.' This can only mean the time when Jesus would make his *last* journey to Jerusalem, when he would be glorified by his death. And the analogy goes still further. In the story of the marriage feast at Cana Jesus does finally comply with his mother's request which he had just refused. The contradiction is only on the surface. For the refusal was directed against the fact that the mother saw the changing of the water into wine as a self-sufficient miracle, while Jesus saw in it a pointer to a far greater miracle which he would not yet fulfil, since 'the hour for it is not yet come'. Thus he does indeed at the time perform the physical miracle but only as a sign of that which is to come. The same thing happens, we maintain, in chapter 7.1 ff. In spite of the fact that he has refused to comply with his brother's demand that he should then go up to Jerusalem, he does in fact comply.[1] Here again the refusal was directed to the fact that his disciples regarded this journey to Jerusalem as final, the occasion of the proclamation of his glory. Jesus, on the other hand, saw in it only a foreshadowing of the later journey,[2] since the final journey to Jerusalem for the manifestation of his glory could only have suffering as its goal. When he does therefore comply with his brothers' wishes and goes to Jerusalem, it is done first only ὡς ἐν κρυπτῷ (as it were in secret). It is to be regarded as merely a pointer to the later journey to Jerusalem, when he will go up to be glorified not at all as his brothers imagine, but to be glorified through death, when 'the time is come'. Finally, this further analogy is to be noted; chapter 7 is dealing with a Jewish feast, and in chapter 2.6 an act of purification is mentioned. The reference to Jewish worship, which will be entirely transformed by the death of Christ, is therefore common to both passages. For the present, however, the main point is that the 'time which is not yet come' is also in this kindred story the time of Christ's glorification in death.

Having established the meaning of the words 'my hour is not yet come',[3] we can proceed and ask what is the meaning of *water* and *wine*, since it belongs to the very essence of John's Gospel that words are used in a double sense, that they signify on the one hand something material, and on the other hand

---

[1] R. Bultmann, *op. cit.*, wants to solve the contradiction by a literary device—by supposing that the evangelist has based 7.1-13 on a piece of tradition, the introduction to a miracle story.

[2] W. Bauer, *Das Johannesevangelium* (Hdb. z. N.T. edited by H. Lietzmann) 3rd ed., 1933, p. 108, suggests that the verb ἀναβαίνειν in v. 8 is to be understood in a double sense: 'go up to the Feast' and 'ascend into heaven'. That would at any rate be in keeping with John's method. Certainly in Bauer's commentary due attention is paid to the rôle of the double meanings of various words.

[3] R. Bultmann, *op. cit.*, p. 84 concludes, from the agreement in the texts which deal with Christ's hour being come or not come, only that 'for all man's perplexity help is given in the miracle of revelation'. But in this formal definition the connexion of this story with the hour of Christ's death is not sufficiently taken into consideration.

point to something quite different. Thus we shall affirm also in the dialogue with the Samaritan woman, chapter 4.7 ff, that the word 'water', besides its literal meaning, has within it another meaning, and in the story of the feeding of the five thousand (chap. 6) we shall see that the word 'bread', too, exhibits a double meaning in so far as there is involved on the one hand material bread, and on the other hand the bread of the Eucharist.

The miracle of the feeding in chapter 6 corresponds exactly to the Cana miracle. The one is a bread miracle, the other a wine miracle, the one a food miracle, the other a drink miracle. When we take into account the fact that the Cana story is regarded as *a pointer to the death of Christ* because of the word about the hour that is not yet come, and when we take into account further that in chapter 6 the bread is connected with the bread of the Last Supper, it seems a most likely explanation that the wine points to the blood of Christ offered in the Lord's Supper. Since Jesus' mother cannot yet grasp this sense of the miracle, he says to her τί ἐμοὶ καὶ σοὶ γύναι ('Woman what have I to do with thee'). That would then mean: you still share the Jewish conception of glorification. My Messiahship is given me by God, my hour is not yet come, when water shall be turned into wine, namely the hour of my death, *when on the Cross the foundation will be laid for the Eucharist*. The wine is a pointer to the wine of the Lord's Supper, i.e. the blood, which Christ shed for the forgiveness of sins.[1]

---

[1] R. Bultmann disposes of this explanation with the remark 'the blood of Jesus plays scarcely any part in John'. In keeping with the scheme which he applies to the whole gospel, the gift of the wine is 'the gift of Jesus as a whole', Jesus 'as Revealer'.

On the other hand the connexion with the Lord's Supper is properly recognized by Maurice Goguel, *L'Eucharistie des origines à Justin Martyr*, 1910, p. 196, likewise by Walter Bauer amongst others. *Das Johannesevangelium (Hdb. z. N.T.)* 1933, p. 46 and by C. T. Craig 'Sacramental Interest in the Fourth Gospel' (*Journal of Biblical Literature*, 1939, p. 31 ff). Amongst the Church Fathers who saw in this miracle a reference to the Eucharist are Cyril of Jerusalem (*Catech.* XXII *Mystag* IV, 12, S. Migne P. G. 33, col. 1098) and Cyprian (*Ep.* 63, 12 S. Migne P. L. 4, col. 383). In the Gothic Missal (Migne P. L. 72, col. 242) we

What then does the water signify here? The answer is suggested by v. 6. According to v. 6, the waterpots are for the *'Jews' purification'*. That gives to our story its worship context.[1] Water serves until this time for the purification rites of the Jews. In place of all these rites there comes now the wine of the Lord's Supper, the blood of Christ. The purification from sin is no longer achieved by following these laws, but in the Lord's Supper in which Christ the 'Lamb of God' offers forgiveness of sins to believers, through his death on the Cross. *That* is the other Cana miracle, pointed to in the physical miracle. Clearly the sacraments mean the same for the Church as the miracles of the historical Jesus for his contemporaries.[2]

As in the passage we treated above about the Baptist's witness, so here a living question in the contemporary life of the early community and especially of its worship is answered from the physical historical fact. Just as there the baptism of John is replaced in the death of Christ the lamb, which removes (bears) the sin of the world, by a new baptism by the Spirit, in which forgiveness of sin is bound up with the death of Christ, so here Jewish laws of purification are replaced by

read 'The Redeemer and Lord might turn the sacrificial wine into His blood as He once turned water into wine.' The pictorial representation in the Catacomb of S. Pietro e Marcellino (Wilpert T. 57) from the 1st half of the 3rd century is bound up with the representation of the Mosaic miracle of the spring, the symbol of Baptism.

[1] Karl Ludwig Schmidt also recognized this in his essay *Der johanneische Charakter der Erzählung vom Hochzeitswunder in Kana* (Harnack-Ehrung, *Beiträge zur Kirchengeschichte*, 1921, p. 22 ff). He however connects the story not with the Lord's Supper but with the Baptism of Christ which is here opposed as Baptism with the Spirit (wine) to the water baptism of the disciples of John. Though this explanation has the advantage that it creates a particularly close connexion with the polemic against the Baptist sect which we have already considered in chapter 1, yet the reference of the wine to the Lord's Supper seems much more likely, especially as the thought is then clearly brought out that Christ *is* himself that which he *brings*, a thought which is rightly emphasized by K. L. Schmidt as relevant in all Johannine miracles.

[2] E. Gaugler, *Das Abendmahl im Neuen Testament*, 1943, p. 8 f shows nevertheless that σημεῖον is only a description of the *reference* to the Sacrament not for the Sacrament itself.

the purification, which Christ has fulfilled on the Cross and offers to believers in the wine of the Sacrament.[1]

One more connexion of the Cana miracle with the Eucharist may be pointed out. According to the early Christian conception, the Lord's Supper is a foretaste of the Messianic meal, to which the Jews looked forward.[2] In the Revelation of John, chapter 3.20, both are seen together: 'Behold I stand at the door and knock: if any man hear my voice and open the door, I will come in to him, and will sup with him and he with me.' We have seen, as you know, that originally the Eucharist also was conceived as an eating together with Christ.[3] This thought of the Messianic meal is also present therefore in this Gospel passage. The marriage feast at Cana is pointing to the eucharistic meal, which in turn is a foretaste of the Messianic meal.

Baptism and Lord's Supper: here we have the once-for-all sacrament and the repeatable sacrament of forgiveness, but both in the same way anchored to Christ's death on the Cross. The evangelist sees this meaning of both sacraments foreshadowed in the events of Jesus' life. Thus, in regard to content, the Cana story follows directly on the Baptist's witness in the previous chapter. The following story also, the story of the cleansing of the temple, is connected to the Cana story in respect of this same interest in the new Christian worship, in which Christ in the sacraments continues his work.

4. THE CLEARING OF THE TEMPLE Chapter 2.12-22

We are now talking about the place of worship, the Temple. We have seen that the baptism of John and the Jewish laws of purification were replaced as media of the forgiveness of

---

[1] In the text about the vine also, chapter 15.1 the evangelist sees a connexion with the wine of the Last Supper. See below p. 111.

[2] See e.g. *Hen.* 62.14-15. Further texts in F. Spitta, *Zur Geschichte und Literatur des Urchristentums*, 1st Vol., 1893, p. 269 ff and A. Schweitzer, *Die Mystik des Apostels Paulus*, 1930, p. 232 ff.

[3] See above p. 16 ff.

sins by the person of Christ, the crucified Christ, who is present
to the community in Baptism and the Lord's Supper. Similarly John understands the clearing of the Temple as signifying
that the *Temple worship* itself is replaced by the person of Christ.
Jesus' words about destroying and raising the Temple (v. 19)
are a reference to his own body crucified and raised from the
dead on the third day. The evangelist expressly states in v. 22
that this reference to the crucified and risen body of Christ is
an example of a word understood only later: 'when, therefore,
he was raised from the dead his disciples remembered that he
spoke this.'[1] Similarly the evangelist had remarked in v. 17
that the disciples only later realized that Jesus' deed was a
fulfilment of Psalm 69.10. Here too therefore the line runs on
both sides of the historical event of the life of Jesus, to the
present in the history of salvation and to the past. That which
is characteristic of the whole of John's Gospel, though in most
passages only implicit, is here given clear expression by the
evangelist. What the Christ of John's Gospel promises in
chapter 16.12 'I have yet many things to say unto you, but ye
cannot bear them now. Howbeit when he, the Spirit of
truth, is come he shall guide you into all truth', is fulfilled
for the evangelist in the new understanding of the life of
Jesus.

The words of Jesus which appear in another form in the
synoptics, and which were misused to bear false[2] witness
against Jesus in his trial, read here as the genuine utterance of
Jesus in the Temple (v. 19): 'Destroy this temple and in three
days I will raise it up.' Whatever the original sense[3] of the
words was, it is certain that in the evangelists' time the use of
the Temple as an image for the community was quite common.

[1] On this 'remembering' see above p. 49.
[2] Mark. 14.57 f par. ἐγὼ καταλύσω. The falsification must of course lie in the
change of person. According to Mark 13.2 Jesus prophesied the destruction of
the Temple, but not that he himself would undertake to tear it down.
[3] When Jesus said after the destruction of the Temple he would raise up a
Temple in 3 days (=in a short space of time) a Temple not made with hands
Mark 14.58, it can only refer to the community of disciples.

Mark, in the phrase 'Temple not made with hands' in chapter 14.58, is thinking almost certainly of the misuse by the false witnesses of a word of Jesus which refers, at least, in Mark's opinion, to the community. 2 Cor. 6.16 should also be mentioned: 'We are a temple of the living God', Eph. 2.21 and 1 Peter 2.5, where the community is called a spiritual house. But, beyond all this, the evangelist sees far deeper inferences in the light of the Easter event. In the words about the Temple, he finds references, not only to the community, but also to the *body of Christ* itself. The conception of the community as the body of Christ, a conception which has such deep theological significance for Paul, is also almost certainly implied, so that the connexion Temple—community—body of Christ is readily explicable.[1] Because of the link with the word about destroying and raising again, this body, as the body that is killed and raised from the dead, now takes the place once occupied by the Temple cult. In place of the Jewish Temple worship comes that worship in which the crucified and risen One assumes the central place which the Temple holds in Jewish worship. The 'glory', the *shekina* of God, is no longer to be found in the Temple; rather, as the Prologue proclaims, this divine δόξα (glory) has now appeared in the incarnate Word. Jesus' answer to Nathaniel in chapter 1.51 also included this thought in its reference to Jacob's dream about the ladder at Bethel (Gen. 28.10 ff). The bridge between heaven and earth is no longer, as then, found at a particular locus, a stone ('this is none other but the house of God: and this is the gate of heaven'), but in a man, in whom the glory of God is visible. The essential point, however, and the point to which the story of the clearing of the Temple adds its witness, is this, that all worship that is founded on Christ is founded on *Christ's death and resurrection*, and makes these events present. The Jews ask (v. 18): 'What

---

[1] E. C. Hoskyns, *The Fourth Gospel*, ed. F. N. Davey, 1947, p. 196, includes the thought of the community in the interpretation, and rightly characterizes the evangelist's purpose when he writes 'he expects his readers to read his book to the end' (p. 197).

sign shewest thou us, seeing that thou doest these things,' *viz.* that thou purifiest the Temple? The answer which follows is the word about the Temple with its Johannine overtone. The σημεῖον (sign), which is here applied to the question of true worship, lies in the death and resurrection of Christ, and we should remind ourselves of the answer which Jesus gave in the synoptics (Matt. 12.38-45) to the Scribes and Pharisees, when they asked for a sign. There too the sign pointed to Christ's death and resurrection. The important thing here in John's Gospel is, however, that the *worship* of the contemporary community of Christ's people has its centre in the crucified and risen Christ, that the *community* assumes *in worship the form of the body of the crucified and risen Christ*.

Now we understand, also, why the Fourth Gospel puts the story of the clearing of the Temple here at the beginning, while the synoptics have it shortly before Christ's passion and death. The evangelist does so in order to place it side by side with the story of the marriage at Cana and because of the remarkable way in which both point to the death of Christ, as it is present in the sacrament and in worship generally. The connexion between the two narratives would be still closer if the evangelist, as is very probable, saw more precisely in the Temple text which referred to Christ's body, a reference to the body of Christ present in the *Eucharist*. Then we should have the same combination as in 1 Cor. 10.17, the community of Christ and the eucharistic body of Christ. Then the subject of the second story in the chapter would be the body of the Eucharist as that of the first was the blood. However that may be, the connexion between the two stories is also obvious quite apart from this. In both, the new Christian type of worship is in a similar fashion placed over against the Jewish. The fourth evangelist had spoken about Jesus' Baptism in the same context and he now comes back to Baptism and relates it also to Christ's death and resurrection, in the passage which follows, which is the conversation with Nicodemus.

5. THE CONVERSATION WITH NICODEMUS
Chapter 3.1-21

This conversation can be divided into two parts; vv. 1-12 deal mainly with the subjective side of rebirth, the effect on man; vv. 13-21 the objective side, the source of this rebirth, which lies outside of man. In both parts, however, that rebirth is meant which takes place in Baptism. There is here a remarkable accumulation of expressions to which the evangelist in his characteristic fashion ascribes a double meaning, expressions which have at once their ordinary literal sense and their meaning for the present. This is especially true of the expression γεννηθῆναι ἄνωθεν, the phrase which forms the starting point of the conversation. It means first of all 'to be born again', and Nicodemus understands it at first only in this sense, v. 5. But it is typical, as we have seen,[1] that, from the beginning, this expression is also intended to have the local sense of a 'being born from above'. This creates the link with the Son of Man, who according to v. 13, with reference to this birth of the faithful, 'must ascend into heaven after he hath descended out of heaven'. This word ἄνωθεν therefore constitutes also the link with the objective side of rebirth.

The relation of *rebirth* to *Baptism* is already a common conception in the early Church. The important Pauline chapter on Baptism, Romans 6, speaks in v. 4 of 'newness of life', in which we walk, through Baptism into Christ's death. In Tit. 3.5, we have indeed a direct parallel to our passage: 'He saved us, through the washing of regeneration and renewing of the Holy Ghost.'[2] But quite apart from the generally accepted connexion between rebirth and Baptism, a direct connexion is here expressed in Jesus' answer to Nicodemus' question in v. 4, a question which reveals Nicodemus' complete lack of understanding. He makes the meaning of ἄνωθεν γεννηθῆναι

---

[1] See above p. 51.
[2] See further *Barnabasbrief* 16,8, *Hermas Sim.* IX, 16, Justin *Apol.* I, 61, 66.

precise in that he now quite clearly speaks of Baptism (v. 5): 'Except a man be born *of water and the spirit* . . . .' Bultmann and some other exegetes think, however, that the words ὕδατος καί should be struck out. But neither textual criticism nor the sense[1] permit such an omission, for it is important for the author here, as throughout the whole Gospel, that the Spirit is present in material elements just as the *Logos* became flesh. But obviously there is a quite special connexion here with the Sacrament. The evangelist knows what he is doing when he uses the expression 'water' to speak of the Spirit (chap. 4, 10 and 14; chap. 7.37-39).[2] Contrary to an evident tendency in the early Church to separate Baptism by the Spirit from water altogether, it is here emphasized that in the Baptism of the Christian community the two belong together: water and Spirit. The writer may be thinking again of Jesus' own Baptism at the hand of John, where indeed the linking of water and Spirit was effected. Just how long the connexion of Christian Baptism by the Spirit with water was found a difficulty in early Christianity is shown by Tertullian, who, in his Tractate on Baptism, bases this connexion on Gen. 1.2, where the Spirit of God moves upon the waters.[3] That which is new in Christian Baptism is undoubtedly the bestowal of the Spirit, while Baptism still remains Baptism with water. This bestowal of the Spirit shows that the rebirth, in spite of being a physical act performed by man in water, is nevertheless a divine miracle. The 'whence' and 'whither' of the πνεῦμα (with double meaning 'wind' and 'spirit') is not within man's powers to determine.[4]

In the second part of the conversation, which treats of the

---

[1] First of all H. H. Wendt, *Die Lehre Jesu*, 1886, p. 261, further especially K. Lake, *The Influence of Textual Criticism*, 1904, and E. von Dobschütz, *Zum Charakter des 4. Evangeliums*. (Z.N.W., 1929, p. 166).

[2] See under p. 81 f.

[3] *De baptismo*, cap. 3. See on the connexion of water and spirit, O. Cullmann, *Die Tauflehre des Neuen Testaments*, 1948, p. 6 ff and W. F. Flemington, *op. cit.*, p. 37 ff.

[4] This 'miraculous' side is well understood by R. Bultmann, *op. cit.*, p. 98 ff.

objective source of the rebirth in Baptism, Jesus shows how this bestowal of the Spirit, together with the forgiveness of sins which is offered in the same sacrament, depends on the *death and resurrection of Christ*, and that in virtue of this, that miracle of rebirth, which to Nicodemus is so inconceivable, can take place. We know already from the witness of the Baptist, where Jesus is called Lamb of God (chap. 1.29 and 36) that the forgiveness of sins acquired in Baptism is in virtue of Christ's death. Here birth of the *Spirit*, as effected in baptism, is likewise based on Christ's death. The Spirit presupposes chronologically the 'glorification' of Christ in the Johannine sense of death; thus we read in chapter 7.39: 'For the Spirit was not yet given: because Jesus was not yet glorified.' In the conversation with Nicodemus there is more involved, however. Here the inner relation between the subjective effects of the new birth and its objective source is referred to the death and resurrection of Christ. When Nicodemus asks how such a rebirth from above is possible, Jesus answers v. 13 ff: 'Because the Son of Man who descended, hath ascended.' There is the source of Christian Baptism. In rebirth it is not a question of a mere subjective mystical event. Again in the sacrament we are referred to the *Person of Christ*, and again to his Person as crucified and risen. Baptism is the Christ event become present. This more precise definition is now given, in that this 'ascending' of the Son of Man is explained, again in true Johannine fashion, in terms of the conception of 'being lifted up', ὑψωθῆναι in its several meanings, particularly in terms of the Old Testament narrative of the lifting up of the brazen serpent, by looking at which all bitten by the serpents were saved, Num. 21.5 ff. The same verb ὑψωθῆναι is used in the same Johannine double meaning of 'lifting up to heaven' and 'lifting on to the Cross' in John 8.28: 'When ye have lifted up the Son of Man, then shall ye know that I am he,' and especially in John 12.32: 'And I, if I be lifted up from the earth will draw all men unto myself'; in the following verse, v. 33, John says expressly that Jesus

77

thereby 'signified by what manner of death he should die'. Thus this verb has here two contrasting meanings 'being glorified' and 'dying' according to the sense. The source of the rebirth which is effected for the believer in Baptism is therefore the crucifixion and resurrection of Jesus Christ, and we are directly reminded of Romans 6, where Paul explains that in Baptism we die with Christ and with him rise again.

V. 16 points in the same context to the vicarious death of Christ: 'For God so loved the world, that he gave his only begotten Son.' Here the verb ἔδωκεν (gave) is used in a double sense: he 'gifted' him to the world, but also in the sense of παρέδωκεν (cf. Rom. 8.32): 'He delivered him up to death.' For this reason it has become possible for us to be born ἄνωθεν in Baptism.

The end of the conversation, which deals with judgement, stresses on the one hand the necessity of *faith* in the objective Christ event, on the other hand the fact that the judgement has already taken place in that event, and therefore that we stand or fall by our faith or lack of it.

In the context of the whole passage this means that rebirth is an eschatological event.

The conversation with Nicodemus, also, therefore, follows directly on the foregoing passages. The thought is common to them all that the life of the incarnate Christ points to the Christ lifted up in death and present to the Church in the sacraments. There follows now a last witness of the Baptist which goes back to the earlier teaching on Baptism in chapter 1.19-34.

6. THE LAST WITNESS OF THE BAPTIST
Chapter 3.22-36

If yet another proof were necessary to show that Baptism is really in question in the conversation with Nicodemus, it could be found[1] in the close formal connexion of this passage with the Baptist's last witness, which immediately follows. It has just been shown that the objective source of the rebirth effected in Baptism is he who ascended into heaven, who in a double sense 'was lifted up'. Now the point is to define the new Baptism by the Spirit, in this text once again over against the *baptism of John*. Again we see what a vital question that obviously was in the early Christian circles to which the author of John's Gospel belonged. He is concerned to show that John's baptism cannot be that Baptism 'from above' which is here discussed, for it was not John who 'ascended into heaven after he descended out of heaven', but Jesus. Again it is the Baptist himself who makes this clear, and indeed in answer to the jealousy which arose among his disciples because of the success of the Baptism administered by Jesus. It came to a quarrel between the disciples of John and a certain Jew (v. 25) on the liturgical question of καθαρισμός (purification).[2] This jealousy of John's disciples shows that they had not grasped the relationship between the work of Jesus and the baptism of John. Their master himself undertakes therefore to teach them.

The reference of the Baptist's speech to the conversation with Nicodemus is quite clear in v. 31. The starting point of that earlier discussion, ἄνωθεν, recurs here but recurs now because from this point on both Baptisms are placed in proper relationship, or better expressed, the originators of both Baptisms are placed in proper relationship; for from the foregoing passage we know that *the* Baptism which will effect 'a birth ἄνωθεν' in man must come from One who ascended after he

[1] R. Bultmann, *op. cit.*, p. 116, has eliminated this inherent relation in that he attaches vv. 31-36 to the Nicodemus interview, but detaches the Baptist's last witness vv. 22-30 as literary creation.

[2] In Sinaiticus, and in the old Latin and old Syrian (Cur.) translation the reading is plural 'Ιουδαίων. The singular as the *lectio difficilior* is probably right (so also R. Bultmann, *op. cit.*, p. 123). The suggestion made by M. Goguel, *Jean Baptiste*, 1928, p. 89 f that μετὰ 'Ιησοῦ is to be read here, cannot be justified on the basis of textual criticism.

descended. The Baptist himself however now explains in v. 31: ὁ ἄνωθεν ἐρχόμενος ἐπάνω πάντων ἐστίν. 'He that cometh from above is above all' and that is Jesus, for he John, is not ἄνωθεν, from heaven, but 'of the earth', as befits one who is only a witness.

For proof, the Baptist suggests to our mind once again the *Baptism of Jesus* in vv. 34 and 35: 'for he giveth not the *Spirit* by measure.' The subject is of course God, but God in so far as he sent the fulness of the Spirit upon Jesus at his Baptism. The Johannine account stresses in chapter 1.32 and 33 that the Spirit did not descend merely to rest for a moment on Jesus but to remain and abide upon him: ἔμεινεν. He, Jesus, therefore, is he who alone can bring Baptism with the Spirit, who alone can effect man's birth ἄνωθεν. He, not the Baptist, is the ἄνωθεν ἐρχόμενος.

We see, therefore, that here also, in this last witness of the Baptist, the Gospel of John has an amazingly contemporary interest, and here too an episode from the time of the incarnate Christ serves to promote the right understanding of Baptism and to combat the false.

7. THE CONVERSATION WITH THE SAMARITAN
WOMAN AT JACOB'S WELL Chapter 4.1-30

This conversation is, like the other, concerned in the first instance with worship. We see this clearly from vv. 20-24 which speak about προσκύνησις, the true *worship*, and which stand at the centre of the conversation. We have already seen, in the story of the clearing of the Temple, that the evangelist feels it important to show that the Person of Christ, who died and rose again, has taken the place of the Temple. Here 'worship in Spirit and in truth' takes the place of Temple worship. As compared with this worship ἐν πνεύματι (in the Spirit), the worship of the Temple is just as meaningless as that of Mt. Gerizim. It agrees with all that we have been hearing about Christ as the centre of worship when here the Spirit, whose coming is bound up with Christ's glorification (chap. 7.39), characterizes all worship.[1]

This Spirit, this πνεῦμα 'in' which all worship is truly worship is also, however, as we have established in the conversation with Nicodemus, the Spirit who effects rebirth in *Baptism*. If the Spirit is the centre of all worship, then it becomes immediately evident how large a part Baptism plays in Christian worship. We can thus understand why the conversation with the woman of Samaria about the living water should follow immediately the chapter on Baptism, and one can reasonably claim that the whole arrangement of passages in these first chapters of John's Gospel is determined by consideration of questions of worship.

Within the conversation itself, however, there is present, almost certainly, a connexion with Baptism.[2] Before Baptism becomes the central question at all, the conversation hinges on the '*living water*' the ὕδωρ ζῶν. We have now enough experience of Johannine method to know that this word also, which means first of all 'running water' is used in a double sense. Moreover this is expressly stated. Jesus distinguishes in v. 13 between real water, which gave rise to the conversation, and that which he will give to drink and which has the effect that he who drinks of it will never thirst again.

What is meant in John's Gospel by this 'living water' (v. 10 and v. 14), a familiar concept far and wide in the oriental world?[3] Chapter 7.37-39 should be drawn on for the answer. There Jesus cries: 'If any man thirst let him come unto me, and drink.

---

[1] R. Bultmann rightly emphasizes, *op. cit.*, p. 140, that the ἐν πνεύματι is to be understood not in the sense of a 'spiritual, inward' worship of God, but rather in the sense of the 'eschatological' worship of God.

The Pauline ἐν Χριστῷ εἶναι is akin to this προσκύνησις ἐν πνεύματι God's δόξα is no longer confined to the Temple: he that is in Christ lives within its light.

[2] It has already been recognized by Justin. *Dial. c. Tryph.* XIV, 1. Irenaeus, *Adv. Haer.* III, 17.1.

[3] See Walter Bauer, *Das Johannesevangelium* (*Hdb. z. N.T.*), 1933, p. 68 f.

He that believeth on me, as the scripture hath said, out of his belly shall flow rivers of living water. But *this spake he of the Spirit*, which they that believed on him were to receive.'[1] In the light of this verse, the connexion of the utterances about 'living water' with the central theme of worship in the *Spirit* in the conversation with the woman of Samaria is quite clear, but more than that, the connexion with the foregoing chapter 3 on Baptism is also clear. While the Spirit is the subject of discussion with the woman of Samaria, we must not forget that this Spirit is bestowed in Baptism and effects rebirth[2] ('of water and the Spirit', John 3.5). The parallel passage quoted above chapter 7.37 ff is certainly to be related to Baptism. The connexion of water and Spirit, which was already stressed with reference to Baptism in the talk with Nicodemus, finds expression in the discussion on 'living water' in terms of an identification; water itself appears as a designation of the Spirit.

We must further remember that the spot where the whole scene takes place is one sacred to the Samaritans: Jacob's Well (Gen. 33.19; 48.22). The words of the woman (v. 12) indicate clearly that it was a *holy well*: 'Art thou greater than our father Jacob, which gave us the well?' Jacob, the giver of the water of this well is quite clearly placed over against Jesus, the giver of another water, and this antithesis is particularly meaningful if it carries with it the idea that the holy water of Jacob's Well loses its significance as soon as it is compared with the infinitely more effective water of Baptism.

Bultmann[3] thinks that it is not the gift of Baptism that is meant by 'living water' nor yet the Spirit at all, but rather the revelation which is identical with the person of the revealer.

[1] According to Strack-Billerbeck, *Kommentar z. N.T. aus Talmud und Midrasch*, Vol. II, p. 433 f, the rabbinic scholars refer the expression 'living water' mostly to the Tora but also to the Spirit.

[2] It should also be mentioned here that it was a regulation in early Christianity that whenever possible baptism should be only in running water. See *Didache* 7,1-2. See above p. 53.

[3] See *op. cit.*, p. 132, 4.

He is right thus far that Jesus himself is, when all is said and done, the gift itself but on the other hand he is also the giver of the gift of the Spirit. According to John's Gospel, Jesus is present in Baptism exactly as in the Eucharist. The connexion between 'living water' ('water of life') and Baptism is made the more credible by reason of the parallelism with 'bread of life' chapter 6.35 ff,[1] where the theme is the other sacrament, and also by reason of the sacramental character which water of life already had in the oriental world.[2]

Admittedly in chapter 4 the writer is speaking of 'drinking' water and that appears barely consistent with thoughts of Spirit and Baptism. The explanation is that water for drinking forms the material starting point of the conversation, and it might be relevant to recall that in many gnostic baptist sects in the ancient world the baptismal water was drunk.[3]

The theme here, therefore, is, as in the conversation with Nicodemus, new birth. Here it appears as birth to eternal life.

In v. 13, already quoted, we are reminded that the rebirth of the Spirit in Baptism takes place only *once* and *once-for-all*: '... shall never thirst.' That is exactly the thought which keeps recurring in John's Gospel, for example in chapter 13, in the story of the washing of the disciples' feet. We shall see that that scene, too, is closely related to the sacraments and emphasizes the once-for-all character of Baptism as against the Lord's Supper, which is repeated.

The various allegorical explanations of the *five husbands*, which the woman of Samaria had had and of the concubinage in which she then lived, are not convincing. Since we have seen that the evangelist sees, in this conversation also, references to

---

[1] This parallelism is allowed by R. Bultmann, *op. cit.*, p. 144. He does not however connect the bread of life with the Eucharist.

[2] See R. Bultmann, *op. cit.*, p. 135 and Walter Bauer, *Das Johannesevangelium* (*Hdb. z. N.T.*, 3. *Aufl.* 1933, p. 69).

[3] See W. Bousset, *Hauptprobleme der Gnosis*, 1907, p. 293, and L. Fendt, *Gnostische Mysterien*, 1922, p. 36.

worship and Baptism, we may at least pose the question whether in the exposing of the life of the woman of Samaria the thought may not have been present that Baptism presupposes the exposure of our former life in its sinfulness.[1] We can do no more than pose the question, however, for in the text itself there is no mention of sin.

Likewise we may only tentatively pose the question whether, in the *meat* which is spoken of in vv. 31-34 immediately succeeding the conversation, there is, in the evangelist's opinion, a reference to the Lord's Supper. The fact that Jesus himself in v. 34 refers this meat to his doing of the will of God and to the fulfilment of the work laid upon him, could support the theory, especially when we consider the way in which the Cana 'Lord's Supper' miracle pointed to the hour of death which was not yet come and how Jesus in chapter 6.38, in the eucharistic speech, stresses that he is doing the will of God.

It is, however, certain that the evangelist understands this story in terms of the very important question for the community—*viz.* worship and Baptism.

8. The Healing Miracle at Bethesda, the Pool by the Sheep-Gate Chapter 5.1-19[2]

It may seem at first sight that we are forcing a system if we claim this narrative also as evidence for our thesis that it is one of the evangelist's chief concerns to trace the lines from

---

[1] R. Bultmann, *op. cit.*, p. 138, explains this feature of the story in a similar fashion but only in connexion with revelation and again without any suggestion of reference to baptism under the title 'revelation as the uncovering of human nature'.

Strack-Billerbeck, *Kommentar z. N.T. aus Talmud und Midrasch*, Vol. II, p. 437, shows that the marriage of the Samaritan woman must have been already regarded by the Jews as sinful.

[2] I have altered the title of this chapter in the first edition (*Die Heilung am Teiche Bethsada*) being convinced by the recent valuable study, based on new archeological discoveries by Joachim Jeremias, *Die Wiederentdeckung von Bethesda*,

the worship life of the early Church to the life of Jesus. We have, however, the support of other scholars in associating this story with Baptism.[1] Thus Tertullian in his Tractate on Baptism (*De Baptismo*, chap. 5) writes that the power of healing which the water had always possessed points to the future remedy for our souls, 'according to the common experience that material things raise us to a recognition of spiritual'. When the days came that the grace of God flowed in richer streams unto men then 'the water received more strength, and the angel (see John 5.4) more might'. 'That which formerly saved one single man in the year, now saves whole peoples daily and destroys death in that it washes away sin. For in forgiving sin, Baptism also releases from affliction.' The oldest pictorial representations of this miracle suggest that this was the explanation at a still earlier[2] time.

We must, of course, be wary of the way the Church Fathers use the Gospel tradition, since they often connect contemporary questions with that tradition on the basis of a highly-coloured exegesis. As far as John's Gospel is concerned, however, after all we have established about its character, we are justified in affirming that here it must be the aim of exegesis to work out the interest of that narrative for the Christian community of the time. Thus Tertullian is not using the arbitrary device of allegory here when he connects this story with Baptism.

1949, that the reading Βηζαθα (ℵ Eus) is secondary and that the strongly attested reading A D G L Θ ar is to be translated thus: 'Now there is in Jerusalem by the sheep-gate a pool which is called in Aramaic Bethesda, having five porches.'

[1] Among the new commentaries: Adalbert Merx, *Das Evangelium des Johannes*, 1911. See also Albert Schweitzer, *Die Mystik des Apostels Paulus*, 1930, p. 346.

[2] The oldest picture is in the *capella greca* and belongs to the beginning of the second century. Left, beside the lame man, there is a representation of the Mosaic miracle of the spring (symbol of Baptism). In the Chapel of the Sacrament of St. Callise which belongs to the second half of the second century (Wilpert T. 27/3), the picture of the lame man is placed alongside two other typical baptismal pictures of which the one shows the baptism of Jesus, the other the fisher who catches a fish. For another testimony from later times see Wilpert, T. 74, 1 and T. 168.

After the previous chapters which refer explicitly or implicitly to Baptism in the Christian community, the connexion with Baptism here too is quite compelling. Even if the story is treated like one of the synoptic stories of healing, it far surpasses them, because it contains other elements or lays special emphasis on elements which it has in common with the synoptic Gospels which permit us to trace the lines of which we have spoken.

It seems, in fact, to be no accident that the evangelist has selected this particular story from among several similar stories of healings familiar to us from the synoptics. In this story, the healing at the hands of Jesus, quite independent of any place, is undoubtably placed over against the dipping in the healing pool by the Sheep-Gate at the 'Place of Mercy' (= Bethesda).[1] It should be mentioned here that just a few chapters later (chap. 9) a similar story of healing is told, the healing of the blind man, which takes place at a pool, the pool of Siloam.[2] At the pool by the Sheep-Gate, where our scene is enacted, miracles had evidently taken place when the 'angel' troubled the water;—whether v. 4 is original or not the idea of the angel of the pool is certainly presupposed. From now on, it is no longer necessary to wait for this one moment when the water is troubled, nor is healing any longer restricted to this one place: rather *Christ now takes the place of the angel which troubles the water*. If the supposition is correct (and archaeology certainly supports it) that 'the Double Pool became, in early church times, the scene of many Christian Baptisms both in Jewish and pagan Jerusalem',[3] then here we have further corroboration of our belief that we have found

---

[1] For the meaning of the name see J. Jeremias, *op. cit.*, p. 8 f. It is clear from the analogous story of the pool of Siloam, where a Christological explanation is explicitly given (chap. 9.7), that the name is important for the evangelist. See below p. 103.

[2] Against the identification of the two pools, a possibility entertained by R. Bultmann, *op. cit.*, p. 179 A. 9 and for the other arguments, the fact is surely important that the Siloam spring is intermittent, see Jeremias, *op. cit.*, p. 9 ff.

[3] J. Jeremias, *op. cit.*, p. 24.

the correct context for this story when we connect it with Baptism, as the evangelist's intention suggests.

Christ in person now performs the healing—and along with healing he grants forgiveness of sin. The interrelation of healing and *forgiveness of sins*, as in verses 14-16, is a regular characteristic of the synoptic writers. Here, however, in connexion with the water miracle, it gains special significance which again points to Baptism. The evangelist has undoubtedly in mind that other water in which forgiveness of sins is gained through Christ. In that act of Baptism the miracle of forgiveness of sins takes place. *Christ's miracles of healing are continued in Baptism.* Jesus emphatically bids the healed to sin no more, 'lest a worse thing befall thee' (v. 14). We are reminded of the fact that, in early Christianity, forgiveness of sins which is gained in Baptism, includes the demand to sin no more (Rom. 6) and that sins committed after Baptism have worse consequences (Heb. 6.4 ff and 10.26).

Finally the discussion about the *Sabbath*, which has a close connexion with this story, fits into the context of our contemporary problem of worship for the early community. At the time when the evangelist is writing it is of course no longer the Sabbath which is stressed by the community as a day of rest but the first day of the week. *The Epistle of Barnabas* (chap. 15.9) explains that the true Sabbath still remains as the 'eighth' day (see also Heb. 4.9) and refers it to the coming aeon, yet in such a way that obviously the Sunday is throughout in the author's mind. The Christian *day* of worship, like Christian worship as a whole,[1] is a foretaste of the coming Kingdom of God, just as Christ's resurrection itself, which is celebrated on this day, points to the general resurrection. 'God worketh hitherto' ἕως ἄρτι (v. 17) which does not come in the synoptics but which appears here in John's Gospel as justification for healing on the Sabbath, presupposes a similar line of thought. This passage may well contain also an allusion to the coming

[1] See above pp. 14, 16 f, 35.

aeon and its present prototype, the Sunday. It cannot be shown with certainty that the evangelist is thinking here in this way of the Sunday; but there can be no doubt that he saw in this story justification for the community's *not observing* the Sabbath in his day—a story which means for him at the same time that all past miracles of healing by water are superseded by the miracle of the forgiveness of sins in Christ through Baptism.

9. JESUS AND THE DAY OF REST Chapter 5.17

Jesus' statement in John 5.17 provides us with the Christological foundation for the liberty He took with regard to the Sabbath! 'My Father worketh even until now and I work.' The synoptic Gospels indicate certain other explanations. In one place, Jesus refers his action to the commandment of love, which can never be suspended, an argument which we find applied to this same Bethesda miracle in the Fourth Gospel, in chapter 7.22. In another place the synoptic Gospels put forward a further reason: 'the Sabbath was made for man and not man for the Sabbath' (Mark 2.27). Finally, in the same place, in the following verse, we have a third thought which approximates closely to the Christological explanation given in John 5.17, where by way of conclusion Mark records Jesus as saying: 'The Son of Man is Lord even of the Sabbath.' It is true that the context suggests the idea that at this place the Greek words υἱὸς τοῦ ἀνθρώπου could be a false translation of *barnasha* in its simple sense, man: 'man (every man) is lord of the Sabbath.' In contrast to most of the other synoptic passages therefore, υἱὸς τοῦ ἀνθρώπου would not denote here the Son of Man of the Book of Daniel. Perhaps the original Aramaic, in this case, did indeed intend *barnasha* in the sense of 'each man'. But the evangelist Mark himself, in writing the Greek words υἱὸς τοῦ ἀνθρώπου, cannot have given to the translation a meaning different from that given elsewhere in his gospel. He himself has thought, in any case, of Jesus as

Lord of the Sabbath.¹ If he is of the opinion that, according to this word, Christ has ἐξουσία over the Sabbath, the attitude of Jesus with regard to the Sabbath finds here a Christological foundation, analogous to that of John 5.17. But the Johannine passage goes further. We must examine the words ἕως ἄρτι—'even until now'. If Jesus declares here that his Father works 'even until now' and he likewise, the words 'even until now' refer to a time when he will be no longer at work, at any rate no longer in the same way. This time would not be different from that envisaged in chapter 9.4: 'We must work the works of him that sent me while it is day. The night cometh when no man can work.'¹

It is the time when the work accomplished by Jesus on earth (and consequently by God) will have reached its goal, when it will be achieved by the death and resurrection of Christ. At this moment, the divine ἐργάζεσθαι here in question will cease. During the period of revelation, on the other hand, the divine sabbath of Christ is not yet come. Our passage implies then the idea that, in the light of Christ, the final rest of God has not taken place after the six days' work, but only after the accomplishment of the work of revelation in Christ, since this work concerns also the entire creation. Then alone will there be the true Sabbath, the true rest of God.

Judaism had already rejected the conclusion which it had been sometimes believed possible to draw from the Old Testament affirmations about the divine rest on the Sabbath day (Gen. 2.1-3; Exod. 20.11, 31.17), as if since that time God was no longer at work.² In reality, 'to rest' does not mean here 'not to work'.³ But on the other hand it would be contrary to the intention of the Old Testament to wish to interpret the

¹ R. Bultmann, *Das Evangelium des Johannes*, 1950, p. 183, has also related ἄρτι with chapter 9.4 and rightly so. But the reference to a time when the work ceases ought to be underlined; in any case should not be identified simply with ἄρτι.

² See Bauer, *Das Johannes-Evangelium*, 1933, p. 82.

³ This is emphasized by G. Schrenk, *Sabbat oder Sonntag (Judaica*, 1946), p. 169 ff and W. Eichrodt, *Der Sinn des Sabbatgebotes in der Offenbarung Gottes (Gott schenkt-die Gemeinde dankt.* 2 *Vorträge* W. Eichrodt-A. Graf, 1950), p. 21.

continued work of God in the sense of a *creatio continua*. It is concerned rather with the work of salvation, by which God reveals himself and which continues also after the six days' work and finds its culminating point in the life of Christ on earth.

The idea that the original divine rest of the seventh day points to the fulfilment of this rest in the new aeon, that is to say the moment of the redemption of creation, the moment of the new creation, is not expressed directly in the Fourth Gospel but in the epistle to the Hebrews, which in so many respects is related to it: 'There is therefore a Sabbath for the people of God' (Heb. 4.10), and in the Fathers, with whom the Sabbath is referred, ever since the *Epistle of Barnabas* (chap. 15)—in different ways it is true—to the future.[1]

But the word in John 5.17, although it does not give expression to it, presupposes an analogous idea. This is proved by the words ἕως ἄρτι which refer to a time when the work of God in Christ will be complete. The death and resurrection of Christ are here regarded as the final goal of the 'work' on earth, and as the point of departure for the 'perfect Sabbath' of the new aeon. Through these events the creation is reconciled with God. In Christ alone, in the New Covenant, the divine rest of the seventh day, the original Sabbath, is fulfilled.

This fact ought to affect our understanding of the *day of rest* which God has instituted, in relation to his own rest. In this way we understand best the Christological argument by which Jesus justifies the liberty he takes with regard to the Jewish Sabbath in John 5.17. Jesus, by his work, brings to an end this feast day by fulfilling the ultimate purpose underlying God's institution of this day in the Old Testament. The same thing holds with regard to the worship of the Temple which he brings to an end by fulfilling in his own person what is the

---

[1] See, on this subject, the various publications by J. Daniélou, especially *Typologie millenariste de la semaine dans le christianisme primitif* (*Vigiliae Christianae*, 1948).

final meaning of the Temple in the Old Covenant (chap. 2.21). If that is so, the observation of the Jewish Sabbath now means a return to the Old Covenant, as if Christ had not come. From the time of Christ on, the change from the Sabbath to Sunday takes place. It is true that it is only the Epistle of Barnabas which refers explicitly, in chapter 15, to the consequences which follow for the 'Lord's day', celebrated by Christians from the new Christian understanding of the divine rest; but it is hardly conceivable that the fourth evangelist, in justifying, in our passage, the superseding of the Jewish Sabbath by the new conception of the divine rest, had not already in mind the *Lord's Day* of the Christian community. In fact, in his time, the day of Christ's resurrection, called in Rev. 1.10 κυριακὴ ἡμέρα, was already universally celebrated in Christian Churches.

When we remember that John reveals a tendency in accounts of all the events of Christ's life to trace the line from the Jesus of history to the Christ of the community and that his chief interest is in the connexion with early Christian worship, it is legitimate to ask whether he does not consider the saying in chapter 5.17 about God working hitherto ἕως ἄρτι an allusion to the new day of rest of the community, the day of Christ's resurrection, ἡμέρα τοῦ κυρίου (day of the Lord).

This day is the sign that the earthly work of God in Christ has been accomplished in Christ's death and resurrection and that the work of creation is fulfilled by the work of Christ, through the merits of whom we look for the eternal 'rest'.

Yet another connexion is evident. Christ's resurrection is the decisive event in the history of salvation. But the completion of it is still in the future, and the final Sabbath rest when, to use Pauline terms, 'God shall be all in all', is still an object of hope. Christ's resurrection is the anticipation of this final Sabbath, of the new creation at the end. For this reason, the Christian Sunday, the Lord's Day, ἡμέρα τοῦ κυρίου is, in its turn, the anticipation of that other 'day of the Lord', *jom*

Jahweh, at the end, of which Old Testament prophets speak. The Christian term ἡμέρα τοῦ κυρίου or κυριακὴ ἡμέρα, which is not found in the gospel but in Rev. 1.10 is the Greek translation of *jom Jahweh*. The words ἕως ἄρτι in John 5.17 refer therefore almost certainly at once to Christ's resurrection and to the new creation at the end. This again would be in entire agreement with the evangelist's predilection for expressions with double meaning.[1]

* * *

If our explanation is correct, the fourth evangelist bears witness indirectly to a theological theory which establishes a *link* between the *day of rest* instituted by God in the Old Testament and the day of the Lord of the *resurrection* celebrated by the Christians. At first sight one might be tempted to think that the primitive Church put in place of the Sabbath not only another day, but a quite different celebration. It was often maintained that to celebrate Sunday would be to disobey the Old Testament commandment which states that the Sabbath is to be holy. One must recognize, however, that the Christian Sunday is the 'day of the Lord' in so far as it is the day of Christ, i.e. of his resurrection. The idea which underlies John 5.17 justifies the disobedience in terms of the divine plan of salvation, since this saying, in basing the day of human rest on the divine rest, considers the death and resurrection of Christ alone the inauguration of the true 'rest of God'. It reminds us that all the institutions of the Old Covenant have their fulfilment in Christ. Thus there is an internal link between the idea of Christ's resurrection and the idea of the rest of God.

The Old Testament looks back to the first creation; the New

---

[1] G. Staehlin, *Zum Problem der johanneischen Eschatologie* (Z.N.W., 1934), p. 244 ff likewise admits an eschatological relationship between the work mentioned in our text and the 'cosmic' Sabbath at the end.

Testament embraces, in looking at Christ, creation, redemption and new creation.

10. THE MIRACLE OF THE FEEDING OF THE MULTITUDE Chapter 6.1-13; 26-65

The long speech which Jesus makes in John's Gospel, after the miracle of feeding the multitude, about the meaning of this miracle, has, since ancient times, been considered by most exegetes a discourse on the Eucharist. The use of characteristically eucharistic words such as διδόναι, ὑπέρ, ἄρτος, αἷμα, φαγεῖν, πίνειν supports this interpretation. Although now and then there have been experts like Clement of Alexandria[1] and Origen[2] who have seen in Jesus' discourse about the bread of life only symbolic reference to the nourishment of man's soul with the Word, the teaching of Christ, without any connexion with the sacrament of the Lord's Supper, nevertheless this chapter is *the* place in John's Gospel where the explanation which we proffer in the present work in a much larger number of Johannine passages has always been self-evident.[3]

Here the author makes Jesus himself draw the line from the miracle of feeding with material bread to the miracle of the Sacrament. That to which the miracle of feeding only points, is here expounded in a discourse, while, in most other passages, it is left to the reader to read between the lines the reference to the sacraments from scanty but carefully emphasized hints.

[1] *Paidagogos* I, 6, 46-47.
[2] *Joh. Kommentar* VI, 43; X, 17; XX, 41-43.
[3] There is in fact considerable consensus of opinion on this point. Of the Church Fathers we can name among others Chrysostom, *Hom.* 46, Cyril, Theophylactus, Cyprian *Testim.* I. 22. Among modern scholars are M. J. Lagrange, *Evangile selon S. Jean*, 4th ed., 1927; Albert Schweitzer, *Die Mystik des Apostels Paulus*, 1930 (p. 352 ff); A. Schlatter, *Der Evangelist Johannes*, 1930; W. F. Howard, *The Fourth Gospel*, 1931; F. Tillmann, *Das Johannesevangelium*, 4th ed., 1931; Walter Bauer, *Das Johannesevangelium (Hdb. z. N.T.)* 3 AEd., 1931; E. C. Hoskyns, *The Fourth Gospel*, 1947.
R. Bultmann, *op. cit.*, p. 161, cannot dispute at least as regards vv. 51b-58 that 'Here undoubtedly the subject is the sacramental meal of the Eucharist'. In order however to be able here, as throughout the rest of the Gospel, to

Of course here, too, the story of the miracle itself contains characteristics which approximate to thoughts on the Eucharist e.g. fish[1] and the eucharistic terminology in v. 11. For all that, these hints are perhaps rather weaker here than in the other miracle stories which we have studied. Nonetheless I should like to underline this very fact and use it as justification of the method I have applied to the whole Gospel; for on the assumption that the subject of the subsequent discourse is the Eucharist, even if this connexion be confined to v. 35*b* and vv. 51*b*-58, which I do not believe, *it must at all events be presupposed that the evangelist saw, as he was writing down the story, a reference in this miracle to the Eucharist, that he had the Eucharist in mind therefore without actually saying so.* I consider that this very point argues strongly against those of my opponents who are willing to accept, at least as far as vv. 51*b*-58 are concerned, the eucharistic explanation and do not cut out these verses. *John 6.1-13 shows what a Johannine story looks like, in the writing of which the evangelist without any doubt was thinking at once of the once-for-all event and of the Eucharist.* All question marks which

exclude references to the sacraments, he cuts out this whole passage as a later interpolation. In this way he is able to dispute the connexion of the rest of the discourse on the bread of life to the Eucharist. That is, however, a violent procedure. The supposed hiatus between this passage and the previous one which R. Bultmann complains of does not in fact exist, for it belongs to the very essence of John's method that the bread of life should be on the one hand the historical Revealer himself, and on the other he who now reveals himself in the Sacrament.

Besides Bultmann, H. Odebert, *The Fourth Gospel*, 1929, has also disputed the connexion with the Eucharist. His contention is based on the legitimate observation that in the world of John's Gospel, above all in Judaism, there was a common metaphorical use of the words 'bread' and 'food', that, for example, in Judaism the Law is described as 'bread'. (See Strack-Billerbeck, *Kommentar z. N.T. aus Talmud und Midrasch*, Vol. II, p. 482 f.) This does not however exclude the *further* connexion with the bread of the Eucharist, rather it makes it the more likely. Besides, Bultmann himself emphasizes, *op. cit.*, 166, that in the same world 'sacramental faith and faith in the word of revelation are often bound up together'. He refers also to Ignatius and above all to the *Odes of Solomon*. One finds it difficult to see why such a connexion should be present only in what Bultmann thinks is an interpolated passage vv. 51*b*-58 and not in vv. 27-51*a*; therefore the rejection of vv. 51*b*-58 for this reason also is not convincing.

[1] See above p. 15.

may be put at my explanation of other passages, should be concentrated on the claim that the author saw in this story as such a connexion with the Eucharist, and the verses which follow, and follow at quite a distance too, 51-58, show that such question marks do not do justice to the peculiarly Johannine contribution.

The discourse falls into two parts: vv. 27-47 and 48-65. Both parts deal with the Lord's Supper; the first part in that it presents the *Person* of Christ as the bread of life, the second in that the bread of the Sacrament is designated more directly. At the end of each part we find a note on the necessity for faith in receiving the bread of life (vv. 36-47 and vv. 60-71). This emphasis on the need for faith, in the context of teaching on the Lord's Supper, contains the answer to criticisms which were certainly raised against the celebration of the Lord's Supper in the evangelist's day. The celebration, as we know, was always considered a most offensive thing by those outside the Church in the early days. In the evangelist's day also there may have been many to whom the word about eating the bread seemed σκληρός 'hard' (v. 60) and who took offence at it (v. 61). It is against these that what is said about the necessity for faith is directed. Without faith, which is a gift of God, this eating of bread has no effect.

When, in the first part, the writer designates the 'Bread of God' 'that which cometh down out of heaven, and giveth life unto the world' (v. 33), he is not thinking only of a 'spiritual' revelation but of the *Person* of the historical Jesus, who in John's Gospel not only brings the revelation, but is[1] himself the revelation. But more than that, we find here too the thought which lies behind all the texts we have studied, the thought

---

[1] This is worked out most impressively by R. Bultmann throughout his commentary, especially, *op. cit.*, p. 168. See also the work by Eduard Schweizer, *Ego eimi. Die religionsgeschichtliche Herkunft und theologische Bedeutung der johanneischen Bildreden, zugleich ein Beitrag zur Quellenfrage des vierten Evangeliums*, 1939. But from this very point of view the connexion with the Eucharist is convincing, when one considers the whole form and method of John's Gospel.

that the Person of Christ is given to the community in a special way in the Sacrament, Baptism and Lord's Supper. Here too we find the writer has in mind at once the historical appearance of Jesus in time past and the presence of the risen Christ in the Lord's Supper. V. 34 confirms that *both* are thought of at once in the Johannine manner now familiar to us: 'they said therefore unto him, Lord, *evermore* give us this bread' πάντοτε. This gift should not be restricted to the single act of the miracle of the feeding of the five thousand nor indeed to the historical incarnation at all, but after Christ's death, too, this bread should continue to be given: 'evermore', not as the Jews meant it, but rather as Jesus did and as he expresses it in his answer: 'I am the bread of life' (v. 35). Since *he* is the bread of life he will never be withdrawn from his own. The close of the verse shows that we are to think of the Lord's Supper, for it speaks of satisfying not only hunger but also thirst. Thus the two elements are there although the context only concerns bread.

Yet a further connexion with the Eucharist is established in this first section. The appearance of Christ in the common meal of the community is of course, always thought of in early Christianity as a foreshadowing of his appearance at the end of time.[1] This *eschatological* emphasis which we found in the miracle at Cana as the foreshadowing of the Messianic meal, is present here in the words about manna and the wilderness. In Jewish eschatology manna is an element which belongs to the Messianic Age. It is expected that the manna miracle will take place in a more permanent form at the end of time. We read of this in the Syrian *Apocalypse of Baruch* (chap. 29.8): 'At that time supplies of manna will fall on the earth. Then shall they eat therefrom, for it will be the end of time.'[2] We know already that in John's Gospel, the sacraments play in the present

---

[1] See above pp. 14, 16 f, 35.
[2] cf. further Strack-Billerbeck, *Kommentar z. N.T. aus Talmud und Midrasch*, Vol. II, p. 481, and again Vol. IV, pp. 890 and 954.

exactly the part which the miracle played at the time of the historical narrative and will play at the end of time. The miracle of the Lord's Supper then, in which the bread of life is dispensed to the community, has its place also between the miracle of the feeding of the multitude and the manna miracle at the end of time. The eschatological connexion which is characteristic of the Lord's Supper from the beginning, indeed from its institution, finds expression also in vv. 39 and 44: 'I shall raise them up at the last day.' It is the body of the *risen* Christ, which is present in the Lord's Supper. He raises us up to life here and now and therein lies the promise of our resurrection.

Before there is any direct mention of the elements of the Lord's Supper or of the act performed, the second part of the discourse speaks (vv. 42-43), within a passage urging the necessity of faith, of the offence which the intelligent person takes at the ordinary *human birth* of Christ, who says here of himself that he is the 'bread of life' come down from heaven. This offence at the lowly lineage of the incarnate Christ corresponds to the scandal that the risen Lord manifests his presence among his people in simple bread which is eaten. That is the connexion between the lowly earthly origin of Jesus and his appearance in the Sacrament of the Lord's Supper. Christ, the bread of life, comes indeed from heaven, but when he descends to earth he chooses for himself the humblest mode of appearance in his historical incarnation as now in his Church. Thus on two counts, this is a hard discourse and one that would give offence, a σκληρὸς λόγος (a 'hard saying') (v. 60). The parallelism between v. 33 and v. 61 confirms this connexion in the chapter, for in both these verses we read that those who are listening 'murmur' at his words: γορρύζουσιν. On the one occasion because of the all too familiar origin of Jesus, on the other occasion at the idea of 'eating of the flesh of Jesus' and 'drinking of his blood'. And with that we have reached the second part of the discourse.

Again the discourse returns to the manna miracle, but now the concern is no longer to contrast the revelation which Christ *is* in himself with the revelation which Moses brought; rather it is manna and the bread of the Eucharist which stand on opposite sides.[1] Christ remains still the revelation in his person, but now no longer in his historical incarnation, but in the Church and indeed here in the Sacrament of the Lord's Supper, where he is not 'materially' but certainly actually present. The manna had sustained the fathers only for a time; it did not bring them 'life': 'they died' (v. 49). The manna was a 'meat that perisheth' (v. 27). The bread in which the risen Christ is present however or in which he raises us to life protects from death all who eat of it (v. 50). The thought that in the Sacrament of the Lord's Supper a communion with the *risen* Christ takes place, lies beneath all the Pauline utterances on the Lord's Supper, in 1 Cor. 10.14 ff and also 11.17.[2] Since it is a question of communion with the risen body, Paul foresees evil consequences for the human body if one partakes of the meal unworthily and does not discern what sort of a body it is (1 Cor. 11.29). The apostle goes so far as to trace sickness

[1] On the relation between the two parts of the discourse see also E. Gaugler, *Das Abendmahl im Neuen Testament*, 1943, p. 58. Although, against Bultmann, he stresses that the explicitly eucharistic passage is part of the whole discourse, what he is really concerned to do here is to show that the more general meaning of the discourse on bread in the first part determines the conception of the Lord's Supper and not vice-versa.

The inter-relation of the two parts is more strongly emphasized by Hermann Sasse, *Das Abendmahl im Neuen Testament* in the volume *Vom Sakrament des Altars*, 1941, p. 57, when he writes very properly: 'there are here, alongside one another, two lines of thought, which at first sight seem to contradict one another and yet for the evangelist belong together in contrapuntal relation.'

Whatever the relation between the more general sense of the 'bread' discourse and the eucharistic sense may be, if it is once granted that in the first part v. 35*b* refers to the Lord's Supper and in the second part the whole passage 51*b*-58, it does not do to suppose that in all other parts of the discourse this connexion is entirely forgotten. Otherwise these verses would indeed represent a foreign body in the whole, and then one might, like R. Bultmann, banish them from the discourse.

[2] In his book, *Das Abendmahl im Neuen Testament*, 1943, where the connexion with the atoning death of Christ and the covenant concept is so well presented, E. Gaugler does not take sufficient notice of this particular aspect.

and death in the Corinthian community to such unworthy eating.[1] But as with Paul, so here the writer is constantly thinking not only of communion with the resurrection body, but at the same time of the appropriation of the atonement effected by Christ: 'the bread which I will give is my flesh, for the life of the world.' In typically Johannine fashion the verb δίδωμι has again here two meanings: 'distribute' and 'give up to death'. The Sacrament of the Lord's Supper like the Sacrament of Baptism is bound up with Christ's death. That is stressed wherever in John's Gospel there is reference to the sacraments. Thus the Eucharist like Baptism is a present Christ *event*, in view of the death of Christ as well as of his resurrection.

The question now arises why 'flesh' σάρξ and not 'body' σῶμα?[2] In all texts referring to the Lord's Supper the word used is σῶμα. The answer is that the *material side* of this sacrament is here exaggerated almost to the point of giving offence. In line with this the verb in v. 54 is not the simple verb 'eat', ἐσθίειν, φαγεῖν, as in the previous verse, but the crudely concrete τρώγειν to bite in pieces. We understand this only when we consider that the main thing even in the first part is to stress that the life element which has come down from heaven is the completely incarnate Christ, whose father and mother the Jews know (v. 42). Exactly as in the Johannine Epistles, in John's Gospel there is a strongly anti-docetic interest. It is a matter of importance for him from the beginning to show that Christ worked in a real body and not in the

---

[1] Hermann Sasse, *Das Abendmahl im Neuen Testament* in *Vom Sakrament des Altars*, 1941, p. 55, rightly emphasizes that it must be noted that unworthy participation is punished in the *body* and that in place of the characteristic formulation 1 Cor. 11.30 one cannot well imagine such a sentence as 'For this cause many have had misfortunes in their work and many are quite impoverished'. See O. Cullmann, *La délivrance anticipée du corps humain d'après le Nouveau Testament* (*Hommage et Reconnaissance. 60 anniversaire de K. Barth*), p. 31 ff.

[2] K. Götz, *Das Abendmahl eine Diatheke Jesu oder sein letztes Gleichnis*, 1920, explains it by going back to the Aramaic בִּשְׂרָא, which can be rendered either by σῶμα or by σάρξ.

semblance of a body, that the Logos did really appear in the 'flesh'. The divine glory, the δόξα revealing itself in the flesh, in the σάρξ, that is the leading concept of the whole Gospel. This connects, however, not only with the historical Jesus but also with the risen Christ, in so far as he makes known his presence upon earth. It belongs to the very essence of the sacrament that the πνεῦμα too appears here in the σάρξ Because the fourth evangelist, unlike all the others, stresses the divinity of the Logos and because he accordingly says, in this chapter on the Eucharist (v. 63), that the decisive, life-giving element is not the flesh, not the σάρξ but the Spirit, the πνεῦμα just because of these things, this evangelist has endeavoured more than any other to avoid the misleading conclusion which could be drawn from this that the flesh, the σάρξ, as medium of the working of the Spirit, is therefore not really to be taken seriously. That is the reason for the offensive manner of speech in 'masticating the flesh'. This offence belongs now to the Sacrament just as the human body belongs to the Logos. The Johannine Christ *wants* to 'scandalize' his hearers with the discourse in order that they will attend to what is important in every revelation in Christ.

Jesus answers (vv. 61-62) the disciples' remark that the saying about eating the flesh and drinking the blood is hard (v. 60) by pointing those who are offended at it to his *ascension to heaven*. What does this mean in this context? Obviously the miracle of the ascension is intended to help the disciples to comprehend the miracle of the Eucharist. Following hard upon the mention of the ascension comes a reference to the Spirit again. For this is, after all, the important thing in the Sacrament, that which gives life (v. 63). On the basis of the ascension, the Spirit is now at work, and in the flesh, the reality of which is to be taken absolutely seriously, although it is *not the flesh* which 'giveth life', for the flesh (in itself) 'profiteth nothing' (v. 63). There is no contradiction between the crude expression τρώγειν τὴν σάρκα and the phrase ἡ σὰρξ οὐκ ὠφελεῖ οὐδέν (the flesh profiteth nothing); on the contrary this antithesis is entirely in keeping with the basic thought of John's Gospel.[1]

The mention of the ascension to explain the miracle of the Eucharist corresponds exactly to the analogous reference in the conversation with Nicodemus to explain the miracle of rebirth in Baptism (chap. 3.13 see above p. 76 ff).

In v. 64, in the context of a repeated emphasis on the necessity of faith, an allusion is made to *Judas Iscariot.* This allusion confirms once again that this whole discourse is concerned with the Eucharist and that the reference to the Eucharist is not brought into the discourse as an afterthought but belongs to the whole structure of it. We know indeed from the synoptics that Judas Iscariot was present at the Last Supper and that Jesus predicted his treachery then. There is something unnatural in the fact that one who has taken part in the life-giving meal betrays Jesus. That is the particular problem for John in this chapter.[2] Judas appears here as an example to illustrate that *faith* is indispensable in the Eucharist and that in this sense, too, the 'flesh' alone profiteth nothing, because in this passage the necessity for God-given faith is brought to the fore.

Vv. 53 and 56 speak not only of eating but also of 'drinking blood'. But here eating the body, the flesh, is far more strongly emphasized than drinking the blood. That is connected, on the one hand, with the fact that the discourse follows the miracle of the feeding of the multitude in which wine played no part. On the other hand, it can be explained by the fact that reference has already been made to the wine of the Sacrament in John's Gospel, namely in the story of the miracle at Cana. There it is the wine which stands out; here it is the bread. Both belong together and therefore the whole chapter 6

---

[1] E. Gaugler, *Das Abendmahl im Neuen Testament*, 1943, shows in his fashion that it is a question of a 'real presence' which is however to be understood not objectively, not in terms of substance, but in terms of experience.

[2] See under p. 112 f.

is to be placed alongside chapter 2 in respect of its content—in chapter 2 a wine miracle; here a bread miracle; but both, references to that wine and bread miracle, which is performed in the community in the Eucharist.

In these two narratives from the life of Jesus the evangelist traces the line to the Sacrament of the Lord's Supper in the same way as he traced the line to Baptism from the other narratives we examined above. We have already seen in the essential parallelism of their content and character, which we have gathered from these references, that Baptism and Lord's Supper belong together as the two worship forms. With the story of the healing of the blind man we return to Baptism.

11. THE HEALING AT THE POOL OF SILOAM OF THE MAN BORN BLIND Chapter 9.1-39

In the history of exegesis the association of this story with Baptism is very old. It is quite the regular interpretation in the Fathers. We find it in Irenaeus,[1] and later on it appears repeatedly, e.g. in Ambrose and Augustine. E. C. Hoskyns directs attention particularly to the ancient Christian lectionaries, according to which this pericope and also the story of the healing at Bethesda and that of the Samaritan woman were used specially for the Baptism liturgy.[2]

Besides Hoskyns, some other more recent exegetes, especially M. J. Lagrange[3] and A. Omodeo,[4] see in the miracle here

[1] *Adv. Haer.* V, 15, 3.

[2] *The Fourth Gospel*, ed. Davey, 1947, p. 363 ff. Hoskyns speaks also, *op. cit.*, p. 351, of a catacomb fresco of the early second century in which this miracle is depicted along with other baptism symbols. The authority he offers (Wilpert, *Die Malereien der Katakomben Roms*, T. 68, 3) does not tally. On the other hand G. Quispel (Leyden) has informed me by word of mouth that the picture of the good shepherd is also a favourite Baptism symbol. Can we then conclude that the discourse John 10 on the good shepherd, which, at least in the chapter sequence which has come down to us, follows directly after the narrative of the healing of the man blind from birth, would be regarded as a discourse on baptism, like the discourse which in chapter 6 follows the miracle of the feeding.

[3] M. J. Lagrange, *Evangile selon St. Jean*, 7. Aufl., 1948, p. 257.

[4] A. Omodeo, *La mistica Giovannea*, 1930.

narrated a quite intentional reference by the evangelist to that other miracle, which takes place in each Baptism.

The close connexion between the two miracles, that of the healing of the lame man in chapter 5 and that of the healing of the blind man in chapter 9, is obvious. In both the healing is performed at a pool[1]; in both it takes place on the Sabbath, and both provoke a discussion between Jesus and the Jews. In the discussion which follows the healing at the pool by the Sheep-Gate in Bethesda, Jesus figures as the giver of *'life'*; in that which follows the healing at the pool of Siloam, as the giver of *'light'*. 'I am the light of the world', he says, right at the beginning of the narrative v. 5. If our explanation of the miracle at Bethesda is correct, then it is probable that the evangelist sees Baptism prefigured in the miraculous healing of the blind man and that with special emphasis on the fact that those who think they are seeing do not come to the source of light, while to those who know their blindness, the power of sight can be given. This thought expressed in v. 39 corresponds to the experiences of the primitive community; it is those who are conscious of their sins who come for Baptism in Christ.

This supposition finds support in the fact that Baptism is early designated by the Greek word φωτισμός (enlightenment) and already in the Epistle to the Hebrews the verb φωτισθῆναι (to be enlightened) is a synonym for βαπτισθῆναι (to be baptized).[2] It is more than probable that this terminology was also familiar to the author of John's Gospel. If that is so then the possibility that he was not thinking of Baptism is almost excluded.

It is also clear from v. 7 that he saw in the event an underlying connexion with the Christological history of salvation. He points implicitly to this connexion in one detail in that

[1] For Jeremias' rejection of the supposition that the two pools are identical see above p. 86, note 2.

[2] See Otto Michel, *Der Brief an die Hebräer* (Krit.-exeg. Kommentar über das N.T.), 2 Aufl., 1949, p. 147. *Ib. Anm.* 2, *Literaturangabe.*

verse—in the meaning of the name of the pool Siloam. He derives the Hebrew name, which really means an *effusio aquae* from the passive participle and connects it with Christ the 'Sent'.[1] As the blind man receives his sight through the water of Siloam, so the candidate for Baptism receives in the water of Baptism 'enlightenment' through Christ, the 'Sent'.[2] In view of the hint of a deeper meaning in this single event, directly made by the evangelist himself here, we are *actually called upon* to ask what it means when a pool of water is brought into connexion with Christ the 'Sent'. To ask the question is to answer it.

Still more connexions with Baptism are self-evident, e.g. the fact that, from the beginning, the blindness of the man healed is seen as belonging to the category of sin. One could find a further analogy not only in the fact that the blind man has to wash first of all but also in the fact that clay made by Jesus is put on his eyes. It may be going too far to suppose that the early church usage of the *Effeta* goes back to the time of the evangelist. It is more likely that the early church understanding of the actual connexion of this Johannine story with Baptism led to the use of the *Effeta* in Baptism. This is not without importance for our question.[3] It is certain, however, that in the earliest days of Christianity the act of Baptism was bound up with the laying on of hands, and in this connexion the double act of the laying on of the clay and the washing in Siloam constitutes an analogy.

The consequence of the healing is also significant; the Jews excommunicated him (ἀποσυνάγωγος put out of the syna-

---

[1] We mentioned above p. 86, note 1 that this makes it likely that in the analogous story in chapter 5 the evangelist knew the meaning of the name Bethesda (place of mercy).

[2] R. Bultmann, *op. cit.*, p. 253, true to his usual outlook sees the comparison here only in general terms—that the faith receives from Jesus who is sent in the light of revelation.

[3] cf. J. Dölger, *Der Exorzismus im altchristlichen Taufritual*, 1909, p. 118 ff, 130 ff A. Jacoby, *Zur Heilung des Blinden von Bethesda* (*Zeitschrift für die N.T. liche Wissenschaft* 10, p. 185 ff).

gogue v. 22, ἐξέβαλον αὐτὸν ἔξω they cast him out v. 34). So also Baptism in Christ involves exclusion from the synagogue.

Lastly the dialogue between Jesus and the healed man in vv. 35-37 is so constructed as to call immediately to mind the liturgical questions and answers of the oldest baptismal ritual.

The opponents of the method of examination which we apply in this study to the Fourth Gospel will not fail to stress the questionable character of the observations made by us on this passage, and we can only repeat here that each detail taken by itself does not in fact amount to much, but that the whole reveals this story, like the others, especially when placed in the context of the whole Gospel, as one which represents for the evangelist at the same time past event in the historical life of Jesus and liturgical event in the community of the exalted Lord. More convincing proofs than those here offered cannot be demanded in view of the evangelist's deliberately veiled manner of speech. Were one to renounce altogether the search for a deeper meaning, however, in view of the difficulties involved, one would be performing only half the task of the exegete.

12. The Washing of the Disciples' Feet
Chapter 13.1-20

This story is particularly interesting in that here as in the spear-thrust episode, of which we shall speak later, in one and the same event Baptism and Lord's Supper, whose relatedness we have stressed in various ways, are formally placed together, a fact which at the same time affords the opportunity of distinguishing the two sacraments one from the other.

As in the story of the cleansing of the Temple in chapter 2.22, the observation is made that the disciples only later remembered Jesus' words about the Temple and evidently only then understood them, so here Jesus says to Peter in v. 6: 'What I do (in that I wash your feet) thou knowest not now but thou shalt understand hereafter.' What is true of Peter here is true of the evangelist also. He, too, recognized the meaning of what happened here and its deeper connexions with the present only μετὰ ταῦτα (afterwards).

What now are these connexions? The washing of the disciples' feet took place on the same night on which Jesus, according to the synoptic gospels, instituted the Lord's Supper. In itself the act of washing their feet was not extraordinary, it agreed with general usage. The only unusual thing was that it was Jesus who washed his disciples' feet. It is understandable that the synoptic writers who concentrated their attention on the institution of the Lord's Supper, have not mentioned this scene, which took place before the meal proper. On the other hand, it is harder to understand the fact that the Gospel of John *does not recount the institution of the Lord's Supper*, since the narrative of this event, as Paul shows in 1 Cor. 11.23, was established and well known since earliest times. Again, however, we must explain it by the Johannine tendency which we are at pains to point out in this work. First of all we must remember that the evangelist has twice spoken of the Lord's Supper in the first part of his Gospel; first in chapter 2 in the Cana miracle, then in chapter 6 in the miracle of the feeding of the five thousand. It is characteristic of the Fourth Gospel that it deals with the Sacrament of the Lord's Supper not in terms of a simple description of its institution as the synoptics do, but by showing how from *other events in the life of Jesus* a connecting line is to be traced to this Sacrament. Thus the evangelist tells us here, where he is reporting events which happened on the same night as the institution of the Lord's Supper, of a scene which took place before that of the institution and which itself only points forward to the Lord's Supper.[1] Here we have a test case which gives us, in

[1] R. Bultmann, *op cit.*, p. 375, 5 considers it 'grotesque' that the Eucharist should be portrayed in this act of foot washing, E. Lohmeyer, *Die Fusswaschung*

this connexion an insight into the individuality of John's Gospel.[1]

Of the various eucharistic concepts, that of the atoning death of Christ was particularly stressed in chapter 2, that of the lifegiving resurrecting power of the Lord's Supper in chapter 6; here in the foreground stands the thought of the *fellowship of love*; fellowship with Christ and through it for his disciples fellowship with one another. When Peter objects: 'Thou shalt never wash my feet' (v. 8), Jesus answers him that only in this way can he have part with him. There is present here the thought of the eucharistic sacrament, on the basis of which fellowship with Christ is realized in the Church. A few verses further on Jesus speaks of the fellowship of the brethren with one another. Both are closely bound together in the Lord's Supper, as in Paul in 1 Cor. 10.16-17 the Body of Christ is at once the resurrection body of the exalted Christ and the community. We understand now why the evangelist describes here the scene of the washing of the disciples' feet and does not report the institution of the Supper; he wants particularly to illustrate *one* concept arising from the Lord's Supper which in other Lord's Supper passages in John, chapter 2 and chapter 6 had not been mentioned. The foot washing scene was admirably suited to illustrate this very thing.

There is, however, a further reason for the apostle's speaking indirectly of the Lord's Supper immediately after the description of this scene. It enables him to establish a connexion between the *two* Sacraments, Lord's Supper and Baptism. We

---

(*ZNW* 1929, p. 94 ff) explains the affair as a rite for ordination of apostles. A. Fridrichsen, also, *Bemerkungen zur Fusswaschung, Joh. XIII* (*ZNW*, 1939, p. 94 ff) finds no connexion with the Lord's Supper but rather a polemic against ritual baths.

[1] Albert Schweitzer, *Die Mystik des Apostels Paulus*, 1930, p. 355, explains differently the fact that John's Gospel omits the account of the institution. It happened because since, according to John's Gospel, the sacraments first became possible after the death and resurrection of Jesus, the Eucharist could not have been celebrated before his death. Such rationalization, however, is quite alien to the evangelist.

shall see that he is very fond of setting the one against the other, just as we have already affirmed a far reaching parallelism in the definition and character of the two.

Verses 9-10 make clear allusion to Baptism.[1] Peter asks Jesus to wash all of him, not only his feet and Jesus answers; no, he that is once (completely) washed does not require to have more than his feet washed. These words can surely have only this meaning; he who has received Baptism, even when he sins afresh, needs *no second Baptism*, for one cannot be twice baptized. The reference of the word 'bathed' to Baptism is the more convincing that Baptism in early Christianity did actually consist of dipping the whole body in the water.[2]

We find the rejection of a second Baptism also in the Epistle to the Hebrews (chap. 6.6), where it is founded on the fact that Christ could not be twice crucified. We know, of course, that within early Christianity there were tendencies towards a repetition of Baptism. There were sects such as the Hemero-

---

[1] The words εἰ μὴ τοὺς πόδας are lacking, as is known, in Sinaiticus, in some Latin translations and in the Church Fathers. They are otherwise well attested.

R. Bultmann, *op. cit.*, p. 357, does not regard them as original and interprets the verse in the sense of a word picture: 'As he that is washed needeth no more washing so he who has received fellowship with me by washing of feet needs no further washing.' In the foot washing, however, he sees represented the service of Jesus which he performs through his word (John 15.3) for his own. There is no connexion with Baptism. If Baptism is thought of it is only in the sense of rejecting the necessity of it!

The passage is similarly explained, without connexion with the Sacraments, by R. P. Braun, *Le lavement des pieds et la réponse de Jésus à Pierre* in *Revue biblique* 1935, p. 22 ff and by Ph. Menoud, *Le problème johannique* in *Revue de Théologie et de Philosophie* (Lausanne), 1943, p. 31 f and *L'évangile de Jean d'après les recherches récentes*, 2nd ed., 1947, p. 56.

[2] Tertullian, *De baptismo*, chapter 12 (also Theodore of Mopsuestia, Augustine, Erasmus). H. v. Campenhausen, *Zur Auslegung von Joh.* 13.6-10 in *ZNW*, 1934, p. 259 ff connect not this 'being washed' but the foot washing with Baptism and see in our story an attempt to defend the baptismal ritual of the ancient Church in which the candidate stood in water only up to the ankles against total submersion. The weakness of this explanation is evident however in that 'being washed' has in this sense no significance which is compatible with that of foot washing. When v. Campenhausen sees in 'being washed' purity through the word that has really nothing at all to do with 'baptism by foot bath' or 'baptism by submersion'.

baptists who baptized daily. This practice is here rejected.[1]
According to this story, however, one thing is necessary,
and that is that for sins committed after Baptism the disciples
should 'go on celebrating the Eucharist in fellowship with
Christ and the brethren. That is the meaning of the words
'save to wash his feet' εἰ μὴ τοὺς πόδας in v. 10. These words
are not in all the MSS.[2] but are, on the whole, well attested.
I hold, against Bultmann and other exegetes who consider
these words a later interpolation, that their authenticity on the
grounds of their content is to be assumed. Bultmann is induced
to reject them because he questions here, as in the other passages, the connexion with the sacraments and for this reason
he finds the distinction of two necessary purifications incom-
patible with the saying that the λελουμένος (he that is washed)
is clean every whit.[3] Bultmann goes so far as to say that, on
the contrary, he sees a polemic on the part of the evangelist in
this passage against the necessity of the sacraments, which he
only tolerated evidently for the sake of church tradition!

In actual fact the evangelist wants to show that the two
sacraments belong together. On the other hand he has to
show here, at the same time, the difference between the two;
Baptism is *once*, it cannot be repeated, just as the death of
Christ cannot be repeated.[4] We have already found this idea
—though in another form—in the conversation with the
woman of Samaria. There is however a sacrament which is
to be *repeated*, which is meant to be repeated, the Sacrament of
the fellowship of love, the Lord's Supper. That is the meaning
of the words εἰ μὴ τοὺς πόδας in v. 10. In Baptism the
individual receives once-for-all part with Christ; in the Eucharist

[1] He might be thinking here also of the problem dealt with by Tertullian, *De
baptismo*, chapter 12 which was evidently much debated in the early Church: why
were Jesus' disciples not baptized?

[2] See above p. 108, note 1.

[3] *op. cit.*, p. 358.

[4] On the once-for-all nature of Baptism see Karl Barth, *Die kirchliche Lehre
von der Taufe* (*Theol. Studien* 14), 1943, p. 41 ff and O. Cullmann, *Die Tauflehre des
Neuen Testaments*, 1948, p. 24 f.

the *community* as such receives part and that again and again.[1]

13. THE FAREWELL DISCOURSES
Chapter 13.31—Chapter 17

The profundity of Jesus' farewell discourses in John's Gospel can really be understood only when their eucharistic character is recognized. This too has long been seen by most exegetes[2] and recently emphasized by E. C. Hoskyns.[3] The whole setting in which these speeches were spoken[4] points to this fact. Whatever the original order was, they have their place at the Last Supper at the moment when Judas, the traitor, having taken the sop 'went out straightway; and it was night', (chap. 13.30 and 31), while Jesus remains in the room with the other disciples, whose feet he has washed, and with whom he has eaten. It is possible that the words about 'preparing mansions in the Father's house' (chap. 14.2 ff) refer to the 'preparation' of the meal in the upper room (Mark 14.12 ff; Luke 22.8) and are in the first instance fully intelligible only in this regard.[5] This would correspond entirely to the time relation between present and future and to the conception of worship as a foreshadowing of the end which is characteristic of early Christianity.

The whole discourse constitutes the background of the Lord's Supper and draws direct lines to the church life of the

---

[1] See in connexion with the account of both sacraments M. Goguel, *L'Eucharistie des origines à Justin Martyr*, 1910, p. 195 f, W. Bauer, *op. cit.*, p. 172 and Loisy, *op. cit.*, p. 388. Besides John 19.34 (see under p. 114) I John 5.6 also compares both sacraments.

[2] See G. H. C. Macgregor, *Eucharistic Origins*, 1928, p. 217 ff, A. Loisy, *Le quatrième Evangile*, 2nd ed., 1921, *ad. loc.* M. Goguel, *L'Eucharistie des origines à Justin Martyr*, 1910, p. 197 f.

[3] *op. cit.*, p. 471 ff.

[4] R. H. Strachan, *The Fourth Gospel*, 3rd ed., 1941, p. 275 f posits the thesis already defended by him that the farewell discourses were composed by a prophet conducting a Eucharist (see *Didache* 13).

[5] See Hoskyns, *op. cit.*, p. 453.

present day. That which we acknowledge to be a matter of the utmost importance for the author throughout the whole Gospel is here expressed directly. Jesus, still on earth, promises his guests a fellowship when he is glorified and tells them what sort of fellowship it will be; he shows them how the disciples will have fellowship with one another and with Christ, a fellowship which arises from this Supper that they are eating. Thus the farewell discourses give us the key to the understanding of the whole Gospel. We have shown in our chapter on the evangelist's purpose, how according to the promise in chapters 14.26 and 16.13 the Spirit of truth, because of the 'remembrance' which he effects, makes possible a representation of the life of Jesus like that given by John's Gospel. When we remember that these words are essentially Lord's Supper utterances, a flood of light is shed on the thesis proffered in the present work.

Jesus' Last Supper and the community's Eucharist, as celebrated in the evangelist's day, are here viewed together. We shall not be surprised to find in the eucharistic prayers of the *Didache* the fundamental ideas of these Johannine discourses.[1] Christ is here still on earth and yet he celebrates, so to speak in advance, the first Eucharist of the community of disciples. The so-called high-priest's prayer (chap. 17) is a typical eucharistic prayer. It differs, however, from later eucharistic prayers in that only Christ himself who surrenders himself to death can utter it.

The beginning of chapter 15; 'I am the true vine', refers back to the wine of the Lord's Supper, even if Old Testament imagery is also being employed. It has long been observed and rightly so, that this passage forms an exact complement to chapter 6. There it says 'I am the bread of life' (chap. 6.35), here 'I am the true vine'. It is not insignificant that the eucharistic prayer in the *Didache* (chap. 9,2) thanks the Father

[1] G. H. C. Macgregor, *op. cit.*, p. 221 points also to the relationship between the high priestly prayer and the Jewish *Kiddush*.

for 'the holy vine of David'. As in chapter 6.32 the 'Father giveth you the true bread from heaven', so here in chapter 15.1 the Father is the husbandman to whom the true vine belongs. The parallelism between these two eucharistic chapters is further seen in the fact that here as in the other a glance is cast at the unbelievers, there with regard to eating the flesh and drinking the blood of Christ (chap. 6.60 ff), here with regard to the close relationship between the branch and the vine, both times with regard to partaking of the Eucharist. 'Every branch in me that beareth not fruit he taketh away' (v. 2); 'if a man abide not in me, he is cast forth as a branch and is withered and men gather them, and cast them into the fire and they are burned' (v. 6).

The similarity of the two passages goes still further. We have seen that Jesus' words to Judas and the acts connected with them form the immediate introduction to the farewell discourses. He had taken part in the meal, but Jesus knew him as the traitor at the time of his eating with the disciples. It may well seem a problem that Judas had taken part in that most intimate fellowship with Christ. For that reason chapter 6 stresses, as chapter 13 does, that Jesus knew him that should betray him. This emphasis is meant to indicate that, for Judas, eating with Jesus had meant something different than for the other disciples. It is indeed strange that Judas is suddenly mentioned in chapter 6.70, as we have seen. But now we understand better that his partaking of Jesus' Last Supper is to be explained in terms of: 'One of you is a devil. He spake of Judas Iscariot the son of Simon; for it was he that should betray him, being one of the twelve.' The text particularly stresses that it was one of his most intimate friends. The exact parallel occurs in chapter 13.10, where Jesus says, when washing his disciples' feet: 'Ye are clean but not all. For he knew who should betray him; therefore said he, Ye are not all clean.' Now the same expression καθαρός occurs in the passage about the vine and the branch: 'Now ye are clean' (chap. 15.2); and this confirms that our interpretation of this verse is correct. Jesus, when he speaks of those who are cast forth and burnt, is thinking, as in chapter 6.60, in the first instance of all unbelievers, but in particular of Judas. The relation between the branch and the vine is therefore, above all, the eucharistic communion of believers with Christ. There is an intimate connexion between the farewell discourses of John's Gospel and the Johannine Epistles. These are, even in view of style, to be understood as liturgical instruction. We cannot pursue this question further[1] here but must confine ourselves to pointing out the strongly liturgical complexion of the concept of the Agape[2] in both the farewell discourses and the Johannine Epistles. The 'new commandment' that the disciples should love one another is founded on that act of love, to which all Eucharists point back: *'as I have loved you'* (John 13.34 ff). Verses 9-13 of chapter 15 offer eucharistic instruction on the death of Christ.

The disciples' fellowship *with Christ* is also based on the Eucharist, and when we read in the farewell discourses: 'I come again', we have to think at once of the appearance at Easter, of the final coming at the last day and of his coming again in the community gathered together to celebrate the Lord's Supper, which is a foretaste of the end—another example of John's habit of using the same word with different meanings. The connexion between this intermediate coming 'in worship' and the sending of the Spirit is confirmed in chapter 6.63 by the reference to the Spirit and in chapter 4 in the passage about worshipping in Spirit and in truth.

The whole worship emphasis of the farewell discourses is seen clearly also in the stress laid on the necessity of 'prayer in Christ's name'. This has its basis there in the high-priestly act

---

[1] We hope to do this in the series *Commentaire du Nouveau Testament* which is being published by Delachaux-Niestlé (Neuchâtel).

[2] M. Goguel, *L'Eucharistie des origines à Justin Martyr*, 1910, p. 209, goes so far as to translate 1 John 3.1 as follows: *'Voyez quelle agape Dieu a mise à notre disposition afin que nous arrivions à être appelés enfants de Dieu.'*

of love which institutes the Eucharist and which finds its deepest eucharistic expression in Jesus' prayer, chapter 17. 'Prayer in Christ's name' is equivalent to the 'worship in Spirit and in truth' to which Jesus referred in the talk with the woman of Samaria.

14. THE SPEAR-THRUST Chapter 19.34

In the last text of which we have to speak, the two sacraments are again set over against one another and here too there is clearly exemplified that tendency which we have traced in the present work through the entire Gospel.

The spear-thrust, which is reported only in John's Gospel, stands in direct relation to the breaking of the legs, the crurifagion, the purpose of which was to expedite death. Since this was not necessary with Jesus, the soldier uses only the spear-thrust to ascertain whether Jesus is really dead or at any rate to make his death certain. The evangelist reports this detail merely because of what goes with it—that blood and water flowed from the wound. Even this observation is not made merely on its own account in his Gospel, but because it is a very striking sign of the connexion between the *death of Christ* and the *two* sacraments.[1] We have seen that this thought penetrates the whole Gospel. The author has found this connexion between Baptism and Lord's Supper and the death of Christ indicated in all the different events of Christ's life. He is able to indicate it particularly impressively at this climax of Jesus'

[1] The Church Fathers saw this (Chrysostom, Augustine and others: falsely connected with water baptism and blood baptism in Tertullian).
As in chapter 3.5 and chapter 6.51*b*-58, so at this critical spot R. Bultmann justifies rather too easily his argument for the evangelist's inner rejection of the sacraments, when he disposes of these references to Baptism and Lord's Supper, which he cannot dispute, together with the testimony as to this authenticity in v. 35 as a later interpolation by the Church. Besides, the connexion with Baptism and Lord's Supper is supported by the great majority of exegetes. F. Büchsel is an exception, *Das Evangelium nach Johannes (Das N.T. Deutsch)*, 1934, p. 174. He describes it as 'not impossible' but 'improbable'.

life. It is important for the evangelist's whole method of interpretation, with which we have become familiar, not only that here the *two* sacraments appear together as they ought, but also that, exactly in the crucified Christ, the connexion of the sacraments with the death of Christ is obvious to all.

This connexion is to be understood *first* in the sense that Christ gives to his Church in the two sacraments the atonement accomplished in his death. It is also to be understood chronologically,[1] however; scarcely is the historical Jesus dead—his body still hangs upon the Cross—when he shows in what form he will from now on be present upon earth, in the sacraments, in Baptism and Lord's Supper, and we know from chapter 6 that this presence is just as real as the humanity of the historical Jesus was real, just as real as the water and blood from his wounds were real.

This short episode is for the evangelist undoubtedly a climax; it contains the key to the understanding of the passages we have examined. All connexions with the present which are seen by the evangelist in these narratives are concentrated, as it were, for him here on the Cross. Only thus can we explain the solemn emphasis with which he attests the authenticity of this, in itself unimportant scene (v. 35): 'And he that saw it bare record, and he knoweth that his record is true.' If eyewitness is particularly emphasized for this episode it must be because it is of consequence to the evangelist to show that this event which includes such an immensely important promise for the present community is absolutely matter of fact. And just as it was real water and real blood which flowed from the

[1] Albert Schweitzer, *Die Mystik des Apostels Paulus*, 1930, p. 348 f considers exclusively this chronological connexion. Since the other plays no part in his interpretation he sees a contrast between the Pauline and the later Hellenistic Johannine conception of the Sacrament.

Likewise Martin Werner, *Die Entstehung des christlichen Dogmas*, 1941, p. 480 ff pursues into the Patristics this chronological connexion between the death of Christ and the Sacrament in his argument that the delay of the *Parousia* was the *cause* of the hellenization of the Gospel.

wound, so also Christ's presence in the water of Baptism and in the wine of the Lord's Supper is real. When the writer of the first Epistle of John (chap. 5.6-8) writes of Christ coming with water and blood, he is surely thinking of our passage in the Gospel. In the Johannine literature the historical Jesus corresponds to the Christ of the Church, who appears in the sacraments. Their identity is to be proved in the Gospel from the life of Jesus. Johannine *anti-docetism* refers to both, therefore, to the historical Jesus and to the Jesus present in the sacraments. When Jesus died, he did not leave his own deserted. The promise that he would come again in a short time bears from now on a new meaning. This saying in the farewell discourses is, in true Johannine style, meant to be understood in two or even three ways; as the return of the Jesus that appeared at Easter, as the return at the end, but between these as the return in the Spirit, as made—not exclusively, but most effectively—in the Sacrament. The service is a foretaste of the end.

15. RESULTS

Two results have emerged from our examination. On the one hand, we have gained a new understanding of the individuality and purpose of the Gospel of John. On the other hand, our knowledge of the nature of primitive Christian worship has been deepened, in that John's Gospel proves to be an indirect source for the investigation of this field.

We have established that its interest in worship is not demonstrable merely from a few scattered references here and there, but from an astonishingly large number of passages which are given a *decisive* place in the structure of the whole Gospel. We have deliberately limited ourselves to those passages in which this interest is most apparent. Nonetheless, even although we think that, in analogous fashion, more allusions can be found in other passages,[1] we certainly do not wish to maintain that all the narratives without exception must be related to the subject of worship, or more especially to the sacraments. I have already mentioned that the interest in worship which the evangelist exhibits with regard to the life of Jesus, represents only one—albeit very important—aspect of a more general interest of the Fourth Gospel; in general to set forth the line from the life of Jesus to the Christ of the community, in such a way as to demonstrate their identity. Because the Christ of the community is present in a special way in the sacraments, this line leads us in many, even if not in all the narratives, to the sacraments.[2]

We find proof of the correctness of our thesis in the further fact that there is a unity which runs through all that the evangelist has to say about the sacraments in the several passages we have examined. The Johannine conception of worship has the following characteristics.

1. The divine presence is no longer bound to the *Temple*, but to the *Person* of Christ. Christ is therefore the centre of all worship. For that reason worship is no longer geographically limited, but all worship becomes worship in the 'Spirit'; even the Sabbath is abolished.

---

[1] We have already mentioned that the passage chapter 7.1-10, should also be noted. See above p. 66 ff. Ed. Schwarz, *Osterbetrachtungen* (*ZNW* 1906, p. 1), in a short note points out yet another connexion with worship: the adoption by Christianity of the Feast of Tabernacles is here rejected. cf. also chapter 7.37-39. See p. 84. Strack-Billerbeck, *Kommentar z. N.T. aus Talmud und Midrasch*, Bd. 11, p. 491. reminds us that at the Feast of Tabernacles water was administered. The connexion between this and Baptism is obvious. See Albert Schweitzer, *Die Mystik des Apostels Paulus*, 1930, p. 347. J. Lowe in an unpublished referat delivered at the third meeting of the *Studiorum Novi Testamenti Societas*, refers to the significance of the Johannine festivals in general for the structure of the Gospel. (14-16 Sept. 1949 in Oxford.) On the question of Jewish festivals, see H. St. J. Thackeray, *The Septuagint and Jewish worship. A Study in Origins*, 1923.

[2] To aid the understanding of the entire Johannine literature E. Stauffer mentions (*Die Theologie des Neuen Testaments*, 1941, p. 25) the later patristic designation of John—the Liturgist. Note also the reference above p. 58 to the representation of John in mediaeval art.

2. Since Christ is the centre of all worship, all the media of the past, which sought to restore the bond of unity between God and sinful man, (purificatory rites, washings, baptism of John), are replaced by the media of grace, in which Christ, as agent, communicates himself in the fulness of the community's possession of the Spirit, in the sacraments of *Baptism* and the *Lord's Supper*, which are the indispensable expressions of the Christian service of worship.

3. Both have this in common, that Christ employs material realities, which point to the Christ *event*, to disclose his presence in the Spirit (water, bread and wine). Although these elements are not in themselves efficacious, none the less they are as necessary as the body of flesh was necessary for the work of the incarnate Logos. Disregard of them is correlated with the docetic disregard of the humble lineage of Jesus.

4. Both sacraments have this in common that in the time after the resurrection they take the place of the *miracles* performed by the incarnate Christ.

5. Both have this in common that they are bound in the closest way to the *death* of Jesus; both chronologically[1] and in the work of grace, which consists of the forgiveness of sins through Christ's atonement.

6. Both have this in common that they are related to the ascension of Christ, since Christ communicates his presence in the Spirit and mediates through the Spirit an anticipatory participation in his resurrection.

7. Both have this in common that they foreshadow what will happen at the *end of the day*.

8. Both presuppose the necessity of *faith*.

---

[1] This does not justify Albert Schweitzer's conclusion that their *Institution* does not go back to the historical Jesus. See above p. 107, note 1. On the contrary, the whole Gospel points to the origin of the sacraments in the historical life of Jesus.

9. The *difference* between Baptism and Lord's Supper, according to John's Gospel, consists in this, that it belongs to the essence of Baptism that it is once-for-all, unrepeatable, whereas it belongs to the essence of the Lord's Supper that it is repeated. Likewise in addition to what we have seen they have in common, each has a particular work of its own; for Baptism this is the work of regeneration, for the Lord's Supper it is the creation of the *fellowship of love* among the brethren. In Baptism the *individual* receives once-for-all part with Christ; in the Lord's Supper the *community* as such receives part, and that again and again.

INDEX OF BIBLICAL REFERENCES

INDEX OF BIBLICAL REFERENCES